Practical Strategy

Aligning Business and Information Technology

Rupert A. Hayles, Jr.

KENDALL/HUNT PUBLISHING COMPANY
4050 Westmark Drive   P.O. Box 1840   Dubuque, Iowa 52004-1840

Cover image from Jupiter Images

TABLE OF CONTENTS

ACKNOWLEDGEMENT AND DEDICATION

I would like to thank God for giving me the courage to complete this subtle piece of material that he has placed in my heart.

Foremost, I would like to thank my wife, Maryann for her belief and -believe me- the encouragements that she has given me throughout this book, have resulted in its manifestation. It was five years in the making and she helped me to push it over the hump.

I would like to thank those wonderful students from my Strategic Information Technology class that I teach at the Stillman School of Business Graduate Division at Seton Hall University for their feedback and wonderful work in editing and adding to the finished work of this book. The finest five that I chose to add to this book are Andrew Joyce, Peilin Hsu, Greg Lubinski, Adwoa Owusu-Acheampong and John Robinson.

A blessed thank you to Ms. Deborah Kendell and Mrs. Krista Converse, my assistants, without their help in editing, making changes, copying, faxing, and printing this would not have been possible. They do not know how great a source of help they has been in this process.

I especially thank my coaches, Dr. David Ireland and Mark Riesenberg. My pastor, apostle, prolific writer (his most recent work is, *Why Drown When You Can Walk on Water and Pefecting Your Purpose*, and friend is David Ireland. He is my spiritual father, encourager, and a source of strength who guided me to the end.

Mark, who I met in the local gym, is also a writer of the masterpiece *How to Stop Whining and Start Winning*. Through his encouragement, I was able to start on the winning way. Thank you both for your involvement in the completion of this book.

Mom and Pop, thanks for being there and never saying no to my dreams.

Preface

Technology is in a constant state of flux and growth. With all its changes, can anyone really manage the influx of technology? If so, who and how?

This is the overarching concept behind this book. If we understand the fundamental concepts of managing technology, then design, construction, and implementation will be accomplished with a realistic fervor resulting in effectively managed and contained costs.

One of the basic concepts of effectively managing technology is the concept of planning. Business strategic planning from the perspective of Information Technology (IT) has been sorely missing in today's companies and corporations. It seems to be gaining more importance as many organizations search for concrete reasons to justify expenses associated with IT. However, only recently many organizations started embracing the idea of linking IT activities with their business organization.

The term "Information Technology" should be an enabler for business rather than a "term" associated with cutting-edge technology. Realistically, the greatest technology created cannot be of any significance to a business if it does not effectively demonstrate significant value added to the bottom line.

In the not-so-distant past we have witnessed some of the greatest cutting-edge technology ever created. We have seen the rapid, widespread growth of the Internet. There was the introduction and popular acceptance of the PC by IBM. We also have seen major advanced technology concepts such as fuzzy logic, genetic algorithms, neural networks, and Xerox's latest Glyph technology. However, if these technologies cannot significantly demonstrate value added or help create a competitive advantage in today's business climate, these technologies will fail and eventually become obsolete.

On a more personal level, each of us performs the arduous task of creating a budget. An individual or family makes a projection as to the amount of funds that will be gained through hard work and toil. Based on the projection, that fund is accumulated, and a present value is derived based on the amount of money that will be received. Then the family makes a determination how money will be spent for food, clothing, a car, family vacation, etc. The family is limited by the amount of money that will be received, and restrained based on the accuracy of those projections.

Corporations are no different. Sales forecasts are made and assumptions are incorporated. Savings based on production are incorporated into the final calculation of profits and losses.

The important element of the family and corporation projection is the accuracy of the assumption and the effectiveness of the planning that is done. Planning ensures that rash decisions are not made, uncalculated risks are not taken, and foolish and otherwise ineffective analyses are not done to the detriment of the family and the corporation.

The benefits generated from effective technology planning will, in essence, drive the business to exceptional gains both from a cost and revenue perspective. Too often the technology function is the first to fall victim to cost cutting because it is a service function within a corporation. It is sometimes done without analysis, but with a knee-jerk reaction from both business and technology professionals.

The alignment of both functions—business and information technology and creative and effective planning—will not only save the corporation millions of dollars, but will serve as a significant business driver to ensure that the company survives in these turbulent times.

If the technology activities are effectively planned, there are significant efficiencies to be gained, such as assuring the investments in technology and people are directed towards improving the bottom line, serving customers better, and outperforming the competitors. Effective planning ensures that technology efforts are business driven, aligned with business strategies, and coordinated across the company as opposed to being done in *silos* (each area of the business doing its own compartmentalized activity). Effective planning will save money by taking advantage of corporate policies and standards and shared services across the enterprise. It will also eliminate the duplication of efforts by utilizing shared services, implementing architectural principles, and utilizing singular research groups within a firm. Effective planning will result in standards for human resources, technologies, and processes; such that the firm has individuals who can transfer between units without a handicap because the same standard is used across the company. Effective planning provides more opportunity and flexibility within a firm. The bottom line is that effective planning will result in an improvement in the cost-savings and revenue-generation of the firm.

Strategic Planning as it relates to technology ensures that the full value and effectiveness of it can be demonstrated to the business. Without a plan, we produce and then ask about value. By taking a step back and planning first, we can look at the business activity and assign certain technology as attackers and enablers. We can also show the value to be gained by undertaking a particular IT activity. With planning, the chief information officer can show his/her superiors the quantitative as well as qualitative value to be gained from investment in technology.

This book will begin a journey by looking at the planning process, the planning document, organizational changes associated with planning, and the changes in management activities that must be accomplished to make planning—not just strategic planning—but strategic <u>IT</u> planning, a success in any organization.

CASE 1 Richard Darman – Royal Corporation

It was 8:00 in the morning on a cold morning in January when Richard Darman walked into Royal Corporation as one of its newest employees. He was greeted in the lobby by Wilfred, a friendly company security guard. "Well, there's never a dull day at this place," Wilfred joked. "Not with all the changes going on around here."

Ever since the spinoff from ChemRoyal Corporation, activities at Royal Corporation had been moving at a chaotic pace. All departments within the company were in a state of flux. Throughout the organization there was a sense of entrepreneurship, but at the same time a sense of imminent demise should things go wrong. Foremost on everyone's mind was sheer survival.

No one bothered or cared about planning. One of the first statements Richard heard at Royal was, "Who cares about planning? Why spend time planning for the future when a future for me here may not even exist?"

He had also heard about the CFO's troubling comment, "When you're in a start-up mode, it's hard to think beyond tomorrow. It's better to just sit back and put the pedal to the metal. Don't look up until things are quiet, and we've gotten to a point where we can say we've arrived."

A secretary guided Richard Darman to his new office where it appeared that any preparation for his arrival was pretty much a rush job. It looked like the office had just been vacated. His desk was completely bare. The secretary explained that his phone and computer would be arriving shortly. After she left, Richard took a deep breath and started unpacking his personal belongings, some of which included planning documents, measurement documents, and visioning documents—materials from his previous job.

As Richard sat there with no phone, computer, or any other office equipment, he decided to review some of these documents. He reminisced about his old job and how things worked like a well-oiled machine.

1. Corporate planning would issue a planning call.
2. Business units would execute their strategies.
3. Simultaneously, IT function/IT department would issue its call to each unit and to corporate functional CIOs for their strategic IT plans. The CIOs worked closely with the business to ensure proper alignment with the plans. They also made sure that current IT initiatives were solid and completely

aligned with the business, and that they were actually enabling the business.
4. By the end of the fiscal year, the CEO would meet with each line of business executives and review their plans.
5. Next, the enterprise CIO would meet with each line and corporate CIO to review their plans.
6. Within the first week of the new year, the CEO and CIO would review the overall enterprise IT plan to justify spending and review alignment with the business and IT.

(*Note: IT function and IT department will be used interchangeably throughout the book. In some businesses IT performs a function of the overall corporation or as one of the many departments in a company.*)

Richard thought back on the comments he heard about "survival mode" and "no plans" at Royal. It made his stomach sink. About that time, James Daniel, the CIO, walked in to welcome him to Royal Corporation. They both walked back to the CIO's office for a briefing.

"Basically Richard," he said, "I'd like you to head up the three corporate functions I mentioned to you when you were last here. I'd like you to approach this from an IT strategy perspective.

"Believe me, those units have never had the support of an IT person. They turn to corporate for help, or they just execute what they think they need. Quite often they go outside the firm to get the latest technology they want."

Daniels continued, "Since I came on board six months ago, I've seen challenges everywhere. As an enterprise, IT doesn't plan. As an enterprise, the business runs its own IT shop. I'd like you to meet with Calvin Trillund, the general counsel. He will be your main client. Also, I'll introduce you to Margaret Ellen, Head of Safety and Richard Smith, Head of Marketing.

"I need you to get these businesses in order from a systems standpoint. I need you to take care of the quick things quickly and focus on what these functions need long-term to make Royal Corporation better."

Richard then learned there was bad blood from the spin-off. From an IT perspective, numerous IT employees from the old regime were now at Royal. According to Daniels IT professionals told their businesses that it was best for them to go on their own and build up their own systems. Daniels then gave Richard some literature to read, and the meeting was over.

Richard returned to this office where his secretary later gave him a schedule of afternoon meetings. He realized he was in for a long day and wondered if he should go to his meetings prepared with documentation or if he should just go and listen.

Knowing there was bad blood between the business and IT, he braced himself as he went off to meet with his first client. Richard's first meeting was with Calvin Trillund, the general counsel. James Daniel, Richard's boss and the CIO, had a dotted line reporting relationship to Calvin Trillund. He began to rethink his strategy for the upcoming meeting and at times was starting to wonder why he had quit his old job.

1:30: Calvin Trillund—Royal's General Counsel

As Richard walked to the general counsel's office he couldn't help but notice the reams of paper in the docking closet. The PCs in the department had not been upgraded for five years and most of the associates had not retooled their technology skills.

The meeting turned out to be quite informative. Calvin mentioned that since the spinoff, the lawyers and administrators had been taking care of legal matters, not IT business. They did not care or want to care about technology per se, but they were interested in technology that would make their work easier.

Calvin listed his IT wish list: 1) create a website; 2) give his lawyers access to information electronically rather than depending on assistants to provide hard copy; 3) stabilize a system that had been purchased two years ago; 4) find out what other law firms are doing in litigation tracking; and 5) learn how other law firms were managing their technologies from a legal standpoint. Finally, he wanted Royal Corporation to have some of the best technologies for his department, and he wanted it at little or no cost.

Richard wanted to hear about Calvin's strategic outlook for his department, but Calvin's focus was on the technology side. Richard deemed Calvin's focus as "low-hanging" fruit (quick and easy solutions) and knew that he could deliver immediate results to the legal department. But he also knew that to focus primarily on these "low-hanging" fruits would only go so far without facing up to the fact that strategies and direction are the next, best, and essential steps to be taken. Richard made few promises at the meeting.

3:00: Margaret Ellen—General Manager, Safety and Environmental

His meeting with Margaret Ellen, Safety's general manager, was no picnic either. As the list of "wants" continued, Richard thought to himself that these folks appeared to be technology-starved orphans.

Margaret explained that because Royal produced many products that go to major corporations and small mom-and-pop shops, the importance of packing and regulatory tracking was paramount. She felt the current system, Royal Safety System (RSS), was a good one, but not strategically focused enough for the direction the company was headed.

She said that RSS was not tied to the order system. Instead, information was manually entered in the system, manually reviewed, and then manually fed to the order system via an electronic note to the order system administrator. Margaret also said that Royal was in a takeover posture and could not survive at its current size.

She mentioned their CEO believed that well over 70 percent of the company's revenue would come from outside the country, which scared her. If the company was to expand into other countries, she would have to report to the CEO that they are currently unable to sell products in certain countries because Royal does not have a proper system to track packaging and regulatory information.

Margaret was relying heavily on Richard to assess the system and report to her on what she should do. She had already started an assessment study with a leading consulting firm and wanted Richard to take over the lead on the project.

A website would be an asset to her department, too. When her department was called for information, this tied up a significant amount of her staff's time that could be used to perform more productive activities.

In addition, employees around the plants were asking for significant amounts of safety and regulatory information. Royal had an excellent manual process for tracking the release of emissions, but the time and effort it took to do so was exhausting. She knew there had to be an easier way. Her solution would be to buy the systems and install them.

4:15: Ronald Smith—Vice President, Marketing and Sales

Ronald Smith, the marketing vice president, was no easier. He wanted a system to track Royal customers around the globe. Currently each business kept track of its own customers. If the CEO were to ask, "Who are our best customers, where are they located, and what volume are we selling them", Ronald would have to go to his deputies in each business and region to get answers. This would take days of collecting and analyzing information. Ronald wanted immediate access concerning everything about Royal customers. "My boss should not have to wait days for information."

"How are we supposed to advance rapidly in this industry when it takes us days to figure out who our best customers are? Better yet, are there any opportunities for cross-selling? If one of our customers is buying products from us at the development cycle, shouldn't we know if they need additional products from us during end-product development? How can we compete globally and expand if we don't understand the cross-selling concept?"

Ronald concluded his meeting by telling Richard: "I want information in my hands, at my fingertips, and so does my sales force. We need to produce information faster."

Richard headed back to his office daunted by what he had just heard. He wondered what he had gotten himself into. Would he be able to make a significant impact soon enough? He remembered what a former boss once told him, that he had sixty days to make an impact. The impact must be immediate, and it must be sustainable. Richard realized there were significant challenges at Royal, and he realized from these three introductory discussions that the company was coming out of its survival mode. Its various businesses needed guidance and direction from a strategic standpoint.

As Richard looked out his office window, he knew the task before him could be overwhelming but wisely pulled out his strategic documents and began formulating a plan.

Tactical vs. Strategic Focus

Richard decided he could turn over the tactical matters to someone else while he focused his on the strategic matters. Royal's Applications Group was a maintenance area available to IT and run by Liz Bianca.

Richard met with Liz to see if her group could handle the "low hanging fruit" he saw in Calvin's and Margaret's areas. They discussed the immediate tactical needs: create a Website for the legal department; stabilizing the legal department's litigation systems that, according to Calvin, had not worked properly since day one; and reviewing the efficiency of the emissions software purchased by Margaret's group.

Liz agreed that these activities belonged with the Applications Group. She would assign them to her subordinates, and Richard would be the main contact person between the Applications Group and any of the units under his coverage. With tactical matters taken care of, Richard then set his sights on strategic thinking and the long-term needs of the units.

Assessing Whether or Not to Plan

Richard's major concern was the strategic needs of all three business units. He felt they were operating on an activity-by-activity basis instead of focusing on strategic matters and developing and delivering initiatives that addressed long-term needs. There were way too many activities in progress. The units were expected to start activities without an overall view of the big picture.

Richard knew he did not want to operate in an environment where the focus was solely on day-to-day survival. At his previous firm the method used to overcome this was a strategic planning process. Richard believed it was time for his clients to start planning efficiently and effectively. He began preparing a document that he could share with his superiors to explain the strategic planning process and all its benefits.

Presentation Created to Explain Planning Process

In order to explain the IT planning process to his superiors and then to his clients, Richard knew his document had to include the process from a big-picture perspective. It had to include information on the benefits of the process and what could be gained from developing a plan. It had to include documentation on the interrelationship between the plans of one unit with the plans of another. It also had to include the economies of scope and scale to be gained for Royal if the business units developed projects together rather than in *silo*.

By planning, Royal could determine what the cross enterprise initiatives were and the benefits to be gained by individual business units. The document had to lay out the process and highlight how it fit in with each business's overall planning cycle. Richard knew that the process used at his previous job could be used here.

After finishing the documents for the planning process, with the approval of his superiors he scheduled meeting with each of his clients. *(See documents on pages 199-200).*

As Richard met with each client, he explained his approach to the IT process through strategic planning. He took them through the document step by step. After leaving his meeting, Calvin Trillund promptly called James Daniels, the CIO, and congratulated him for hiring someone who focused on long-term plans rather than short-term gain.

Margaret from Safety immediately saw the value to be gained from planning. If she knew when the systems would be in, she could better communicate with the CEO the timing of completion of regulatory documents for various countries in which Royal wanted to sell.

Ronald from Marketing was not as easily convinced. He wanted movement on his project, and he wanted it immediately. He felt that if they embarked on Richard's IT process, it could turn out to be a waste of time. Richard explained to Ronald that there was actually much more to gain if they took on the planning activity. He also explained that with the plans he would be better able to communicate to his higher-ups what his deliverables would be and when. He was eventually able to get Ronald to at least go through the first iteration of planning.

Planning Meeting and Plan Development

After getting his three clients on board, Richard then scheduled a planning meeting with each business unit: Legal, Safety, and Marketing.
The first meeting with each unit was a bit tense because it was the first time that this type of planning activity had occurred at Royal. The participants did not know what to expect.

Richard had insisted that in order to complete the plan effectively and successfully, the highest-level person responsible for the budgets needed to be at the meeting. Key decision-makers also needed to be present so there would be little time wasted on efforts where units lacked budget or support.

Once again he met separately with Safety, Legal, and then Marketing, and utilized the same process for all three areas. For each meeting Richard first met with various groups to gather information and later present to the whole group and upper management. The planning meeting to present his findings lasted anywhere from eight to sixteen hours—depending on the department.

Normally, the morning session was dedicated to developing the strategies and objectives for the unit and the initiative planning for the upcoming year. The afternoon session was dedicated to creating and working on Key Initiatives for the upcoming year. Richard facilitated the meeting and the agenda went as follows:

8:30 a.m.	*Breakfast*
8:45 a.m.	Introduction
9:00 a.m.	Business Unit Mission
	Business Unit Goals
	Business Unit Objectives
10:00 a.m.	*Break*

> Business Unit Strategies and Processes
> Strategic Alignment Issues and Gaps
> Compliance and Regulatory Issues affecting Strategy
> Three-Year Initiative View

12:00 p.m.	*Lunch*
1:00 p.m.	Strategic Business Technology Alignment
	Strategic IT Alignment
2:30 p.m.	*Break*
	Strategic Business – IT Initiative Alignment
4:00 p.m.	The One-Year Picture
	Potential Budgets Issues
5:00 p.m.	*Dismiss*

A flow of the process and actions taken during a typical planning session occurred as follows:

- ***Document the business/service units goals, objectives, missions, strategies***: In Safety, for example, Margaret had previously met offsite with her direct reports to gather information related to their Unit. She focused on the message delivered to her from the CEO, which was that Royal was expanding rapidly into foreign markets and they needed systems that supported the overall goals of the corporation. Richard drafted that information on the board and on paper.

- Richard then created a list of the unit's initiatives and placed them on a three-year agenda. This would be confirmed at the review meeting. Richard asked each participant around the table if they had unlimited budgets and resources, and what potential initiatives they would like the unit to have. This was done independent of a timeline.

- He linked the business objectives with the IT strategies using the strategic business technology alignment table.

- He linked the ***IT strategies to the various IT initiatives*** by utilizing the strategic IT alignment table.

- Next, he linked the IT Initiatives back to ***the business objectives by using the strategic business alignment table***. The linking of the objectives to the strategies to the initiative was not quite as painful as initially anticipated. The painful process, however, was getting from the units their overall feel for how important the specific initiative was to particular business objectives. Richard knew that the utilization of this process would make it a lot easier to prioritize the initiatives. He knew there were some people present who had emotional attachments to some of the initiatives. By using the table, the emotions were removed from the process, leaving just the "bare" facts.

- He proceeded to develop the one-year picture and from there, drafted the Key Initiatives List and Categorization.

In addition to the planning activity during planning meeting, Richard performed various tasks on his own:

- He called his lower-level direct reports and spoke directly to vendors to gather information on cost, current technologies, and resources. He needed to find out what it would take to complete the initiatives.

- His next step was to determine gaps in the process from where the organization was to where it was headed, both from an IT and business perspective.

- He met with the chief technology officer to determine the future of the firm with respect to the basic technologies already used on a daily basis and to future technologies Royal would be using.

- He met with the head of Maintenance Systems to help develop the current architecture.

- The final section of the business systems plan dealt with the IT landscape and strategies. There Richard documented the support he had, common technologies being used, and possible shared technologies that he believed could be used across the organization.

Review

Once Richard had gathered all the details, he developed a presentation document that included all the parts of the Business Systems Plan. The document was clear, precise, and developed with executive management in mind. He gave a copy to his boss for review. Next, both men met with James Daniel, the CIO, who reviewed the presentation and made some changes, but in general agreed with its content.

Richard then scheduled meetings with Calvin Trillund, Margaret Elle, and Richard Smith to review their documents respectively for each unit. The reviews went well and became an iterative process as each person made changes with respect to their own budgets. Some items were included, and some were taken off the table based on the prioritization matrix used in the working session.

The CIO and all the business leaders were pleased with the results. They not only had information on the direction each unit was headed, but they had a sense of the timing and the possible resources that would be required. This information was very helpful and served to increase the value of the information that they had to share with the CFO and the CEO.

Richard now knew what his agenda looked like for the upcoming years and was ready to move. Back in his office, he looked out the window across the way. He wondered why in his mind he had questioned coming to Royal. He was now satisfied and ready to execute.

Presentation for Planning Process Documents I

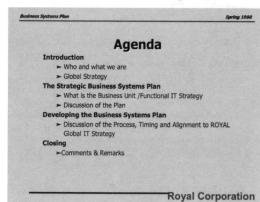

Agenda

Introduction
- ➤ Who and what we are
- ➤ Global Strategy

The Strategic Business Systems Plan
- ➤ What is the Business Unit /Functional IT Strategy
- ➤ Discussion of the Plan

Developing the Business Systems Plan
- ➤ Discussion of the Process, Timing and Alignment to ROYAL Global IT Strategy

Closing
- ➤Comments & Remarks

Royal Corporation

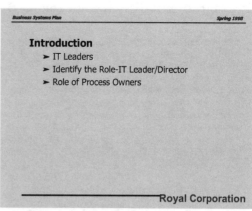

Introduction
- ➤ IT Leaders
- ➤ Identify the Role-IT Leader/Director
- ➤ Role of Process Owners

Royal Corporation

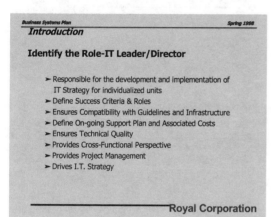

Introduction

Identify the Role-IT Leader/Director

- ➤ Responsible for the development and implementation of IT Strategy for individualized units
- ➤ Define Success Criteria & Roles
- ➤ Ensures Compatibility with Guidelines and Infrastructure
- ➤ Define On-going Support Plan and Associated Costs
- ➤ Ensures Technical Quality
- ➤ Provides Cross-Functional Perspective
- ➤ Provides Project Management
- ➤ Drives I.T. Strategy

Royal Corporation

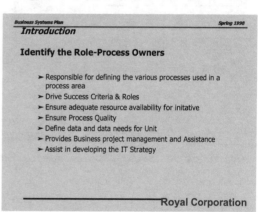

Introduction

Identify the Role-Process Owners

- ➤ Responsible for defining the various processes used in a process area
- ➤ Drive Success Criteria & Roles
- ➤ Ensure adequate resource availability for initative
- ➤ Ensure Process Quality
- ➤ Define data and data needs for Unit
- ➤ Provides Business project management and Assistance
- ➤ Assist in developing the IT Strategy

Royal Corporation

Introduction

➤ **To Become a Global Company**

- ➤ No longer silo focus
- ➤ Interaction and integration between systems and businesses is a requirement (not only locally, but globally)
- ➤ Strategically the mode of operation for a business in silo is not supported in this new environment
- ➤ ROYAL continues to expand operations globally
- ➤ New resources and plans must be implemented to address the changing and evolving global business landscape
- ➤ We are here to talk about activities to address this overall change

Royal Corporation

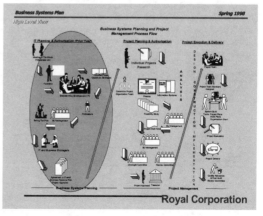

Royal Corporation

Presentation for Planning Process Documents (cont.)

Slide 1

Business Systems Plan   *Spring 1998*

The Strategic Business Systems Plan
- ➤ Planning and Why
- ➤ Business Unit Functional/IT Strategy
- ➤ Plan Structure - Form & Content
- ➤ Planning Tools

Royal Corporation

Slide 2

Business Systems Plan   *Spring 1998*

The Strategic Business Systems Plan

Planning and Why? - Quotes

"We don't need the plan done, why don't we start reviewing the options for the new software"

"Start working on the project, we will find out what the users want and then we will plan for it"

"Let's start the project. We know what the users want"

"Let's just do what we have to to do. It might be a throw-away. We are not sure of what the cost, but in the long run, it might be a throw away"

Royal Corporation

Slide 3

Business Systems Plan   *Spring 1998*

The Strategic Business Systems Plan

Plan Structure - Content

ROYAL INITIATIVE JUSTIFICATION

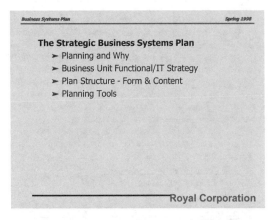

BUSINESS OBJECTIVES ⟹ IT STRATEGIES ⟹ IT INITIATIVES

EVERY IT INITIATIVE NEEDS TO BE LINKED TO A BUSINESS OBJECTIVE

Royal Corporation

Slide 4

Business Systems Plan   *Spring 1998*

The Strategic Business Systems Plan

Business Unit Functional/IT Strategy
- ➤ Each unit will be performing the *"strategizing/planning"* activities both for Business and Information Technology
- ➤ Focus of planning within units is to align the IT agenda with the business agenda
- ➤ Understanding and knowing the business in which we operate will be key to success
- ➤ As IT Leaders we need to demonstrate to the business leader need for alignment and to have a singular focus view in terms of organizational direction
- ➤ Focusing on strategy and planning will in the long run lower costs, reduce redundancies and increase relationships and cooperation between the Business and Information Technology entities

Royal Corporation

Slide 5

Business Systems Plan   *Spring 1998*

The Strategic Business Systems Plan

Plan Structure - Form & Content

BSP: BUSINESS ENVIRONMENT & STRATEGIES

BSP: SYSTEMS OVERVIEW

BSP: KEY INITIATIVES LIST
1.
2.
3.
4.
5.

INITIATIVE 1
   2
    3
     4

BSP: Summary of program characteristics

Program characteristics important for coordination and measurement.
(Approximations where appropriate)

	Business Justification	Important Technologies	Schedule estimates	Resources required	$ Estimated /allocated
Initiative 1.					
Initiative 2.					
Initiative 3.					
Initiative 4.					
Initiative x.					

Royal Corporation

Slide 6

Business Systems Plan   *Spring 1998*

The Strategic Business Systems Plan

Plan Structure - Form
- Executive Summary
  - Overview of the entire document
  - Strategic, other development, infrastructure, business as usual, year 2000, and chargeback costs
  - Resource and costs estimates
- Strategies and Objectives
  - Capture Business Unit's Mission, Goals, Objectives and Strategies
  - Key Information Technology Strategies to enable the business
- Initiative Planning
  - Devising the overall initiatives to support the mission, goals, objectives and strategy of the Business Unit
  - Start developing your three year plan
- Key Initiatives For The Coming Year
  - Devise a list of initiative list and categorization
  - Devise a pictorial View – One Year Plan
- Business Unit IT Landscape & Strategies
  - Overall technology direction for your department
  - Progress planned towards the target environment
- Potential Key Initiatives
  - Major initiatives that did not make the "cut" Alternative means to launch these initiatives

Royal Corporation

Presentation for Planning Process Documents (cont.)

Business Systems Plan — *Spring 1998*

The Strategic Business Systems Plan
Plan Structure - Content
- **Executive Summary**
  - Business Systems Plan Overview
  - Information Technology Budget Expectation and Categorization
  - Key Initiatives List and Requirements
  - Compliance and External Regulatory Initiatives
  - Other Important Items

Royal Corporation

Business Systems Plan — *Spring 1998*

The Strategic Business Systems Plan
Plan Structure - Content
- **Strategies and Objectives**
  - Business Unit's Mission
  - Business Unit's Goals
  - Business Unit's Objectives
  - Business Unit's Strategies/Processes
  - Key Information Technology Strategies
  - Strategic Alignment Issues/Gaps
  - Strategic Business Technology Alignment

Royal Corporation

Business Systems Plan — *Spring 1998*

The Strategic Business Systems Plan
Plan Structure - Content
- **Initiatives Planning**
  - Strategic IT Alignment
  - Strategic Business Alignment
  - Pictorial View – Three Year Plan
  - System Architecture Diagram
- **Key Initiatives For The Coming Year**
  - Key Initiatives List and Categorization
  - Pictorial View – One Year Plan
  - Key Initiative(s)
  - Strategic Themes

Royal Corporation

Business Systems Plan — *Spring 1998*

The Strategic Business Systems Plan
Plan Structure - Content

ROYAL INITIATIVE JUSTIFICATION

BUSINESS OBJECTIVES ⟹ **IT STRATEGIES** ⟹ **IT INITIATIVES**

EVERY IT INITIATIVE NEEDS TO BE LINKED TO A BUSINESS OBJECTIVE

Royal Corporation

Business Systems Plan — *Spring 1998*

The Strategic Business Systems Plan
Plan Structure - Content

IT Strategies	Business Objectives									
	Objective 1	Objective 2	Objective 3	Objective 4	Objective 5	Objective 6	Objective 7	Objective 8	Objective 9	Objective 10
IT Strategies 1										
IT Strategies 2										
IT Strategies 3										
IT Strategies 4										
IT Strategies 5										
IT Strategies 6										
IT Strategies 7										
IT Strategies 8										
IT Strategies 9										
IT Strategies 10										
IT Strategies 11										
IT Strategies 12										
IT Strategies 13										
IT Strategies 14										
IT Strategies 15										

Royal Corporation

Business Systems Plan — *Spring 1998*

The Strategic Business Systems Plan
Plan Structure - Content

Initiatives	Information Technology Strategies									
	IT Strategy 1	IT Strategy 2	IT Strategy 3	IT Strategy 4	IT Strategy 5	IT Strategy 6	IT Strategy 7	IT Strategy 8	IT Strategy 9	IT Strategy 10
Initiative 1										
Initiative 2										
Initiative 3										
Initiative 4										
Initiative 5										
Initiative 6										
Initiative 7										
Initiative 8										
Initiative 9										
Initiative 10										
Initiative 11										
Initiative 12										
Initiative 13										
Initiative 14										
Initiative 15										

Royal Corporation

Presentation for Planning Process Documents (cont.)

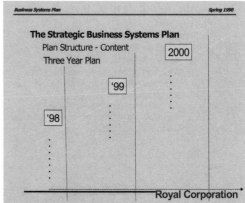

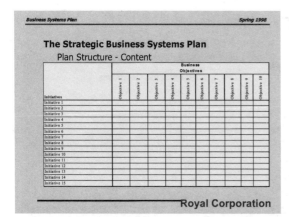

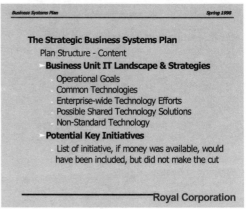

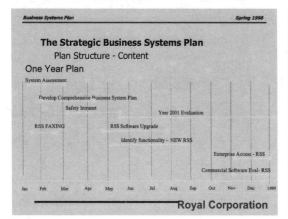

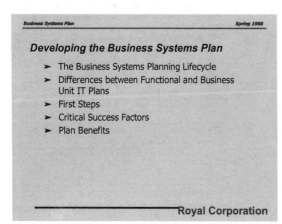

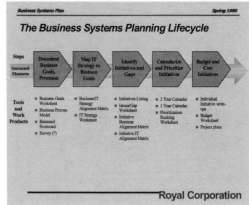

1 Understanding Information Technology

1.1 High-Level View of IT

An alarming number of today's business professionals lack a basic understanding of how information technology (IT) functions in a business. According to Gartner Group, the country's premier IT consulting research company, there are two major obstacles: 1) a lack of understanding of the value of IT, and 2) a failure of alignment of IT within their business.

The way to address Gartner Group's findings is to take a step back and focus on the planning activities that are needed for successful execution and implementation of technology. By focusing on planning, we will be able to: 1) demonstrate how leaders can align IT within their own business environment, 2) educate business professionals on how easy it is to understand technology operations in their business environment, and 3) capitalize on the use of technology through effective planning.

There have been many books and magazine articles written on the topic of "planning" as it relates to the overall operation of information technology departments in various businesses. We know that fundamentally, most IT groups regardless of their industry all operate in basically the same manner. In financial services and pharmaceutical industries, for example speed is rather important and using technology, to enable and drive the business is paramount. In the chemical industry, on the other hand, things move a bit slower. This ensures that the business benefits are derived, calculated, and audited before delivery.

In any case, technology operations are basically the same across the board. How IT operates is still the same. At the highest level, each technology department builds, buys, or supports activities. The important factor is that the infrastructure existing behind the technology activities drives it to its ultimate goal of customer satisfaction.

To understand information technology operation in its entirety, it is crucial that we take a step back and focus on the big picture or the high-level view[1] of technology development and execution. We will begin the process by taking a "god-like" view from space of the world of information technology and further subdivide the world into various countries, which in this case we will call components. Taking the information technology world in which one will operate and breaking it into components, we will observe that there are about fourteen (14) components of the overall operating picture of information technology. Let's take a high-level view at this in the following diagram and further examine each component part for clarity.

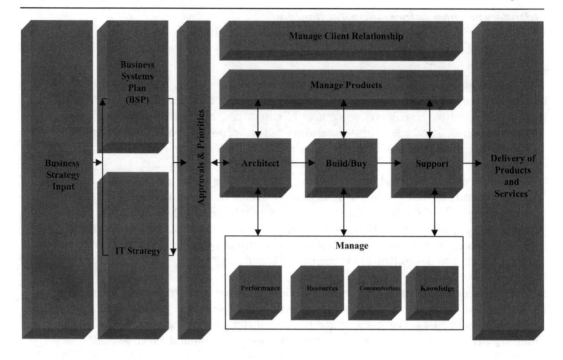

Figure 1.1. 1   High-Level View of IT

Business Strategy Input. In terms of process operation, the IT function should expect to have its activities driven by the business. Consequently, recent trends indicate that most chief information officers (CIO) and senior IT directors drive home the point that the IT group will take its lead from the "customer" they serve: the business.

If IT takes its lead from the business, then the expectations are that each IT initiative should be aligned and tied to a business activity. This leads to the Information Technology overall mantra, which I call the *Alignment Link.*

Figure 1.1. 1a.   Business Strategy Input

Figure 1.1. 2   The Alignment Link

The Alignment Link, if implemented and utilized correctly, can help IT professionals focus not just on technology for technology's sake, but the usage of technology to enhance and further the business. With this type of balanced focus on the business, then IT will not only perform its initiatives, but will also look to the business to be a driver of what it does.

Therefore from an operational standpoint, the first and most important aspect of IT development is its reliance on their firm's business strategy. Information technology should not move forward without a clear, concise understanding of the current environment it supports and the goals, mission, objectives, etc., therein. This approach is discussed in a later chapter.

A few good books that describe in detail the technical development and formulation of a Business Strategy are *The Strategy Concept and Process: A Pragmatic Approach* by Arnoldo C. Hax and Nicolas S. Majluf, and *The Strategy Process: Concepts, Contexts, Cases* by Henry Mintzberg and James Brian Quinn.

The purpose of this book is not to go into the technical development of the strategy, but to outline how it is done and how the IT professional should be aware of this process in the overall technology operation.

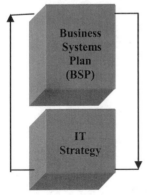

IT Strategy and Business Systems Plan. With a clear understanding of the business direction, most IT professionals can move forward and create an information technology strategy. This is a detailed roadmap from a technology standpoint showing the direction of the IT function.

There has been much discussion on the relevancy of the information technology strategy and the business systems plan (BSP). In my view, the BSP could be used as the sole direction document for the IT function.

Figure 1.1. 3   IT Strategy & Business Systems Plan

What I have discovered, however, is that most IT strategy direction documents are so technical that the business partners wonder just what they are.

Most IT strategic documents are for the IT professional and should be kept away from the business. The BSP, however, is a more "business-friendly" document that focuses initially on the mission, goals, objectives, strategies, and aspirations of the business. The BSP takes into consideration the Alignment Link, which should be a driver for most IT initiatives. We will discuss the BSP in more detail later.

Approval and Priorities

After determining what the IT landscape is and that there is sufficient alignment of the business with the IT function, there are usually "sign-off ceremonies." This is where business and IT leaders meet to agree on IT activities for the upcoming year.

The reason for the short time span for future IT planning (one to three years) is because of technology's rapidly changing nature. In the 1960s to mid-1970s, IT plans and strategies were generated on a five-to-seven-year horizon. That changed drastically with the introduction of the PC in the early 1980s and accelerated with the advent of the Internet.

Figure 1.1. 3a Approval and Priorities

The interesting activity surrounding such events is that there are two drivers of this acceleration. First, the technology itself, and the speed at which computers process information. Second, and more critical was the acceptance and use of technology-related products and services. The more users wanted, the more technologists were able to deliver. There is no difference between what goes on in society and what goes on in a corporation. The business will always seek more advanced uses of technology, and the IT department must be able to deliver.

The agreement on the time span must be driven by the business, but guided by IT. The determination is then made as to the prioritization of IT activities for the upcoming year. Without this step, the IT function will operate in a state of organized chaos—the function knows what it needs to deliver on a monthly basis, but that constantly changes based on the needs of lower-level users. When those needs are taken on, it can disrupt the IT portfolio. This can eventually lead to user dissatisfaction at the non-delivery of IT projects-or, what I call the "customer service death spiral" (CSDS).

The spiral begins as follows: at the beginning of the year, IT and the business agree to a list of IT initiatives that will be undertaken by the IT function. Members of the IT functions are taught to be very customer-focused. They accept this challenge by accommodating all requests from users. Each time the user requests a change or an implementation activity, the IT function accepts the new assignment or project and adds it to the portfolio. Because the IT function is operating with limited resources and a fixed timeline, each new project disrupts the portfolio and creates a resource drain on the projects already in progress.

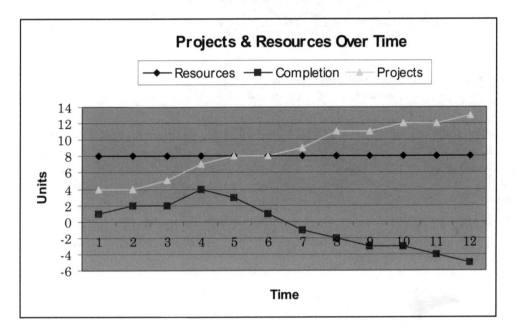

Figure 1.1. 4   Projects and Resources Over Time

Optimally, the IT function would have been able to sustain project development with a fixed amount of resources over a fixed time frame. Optimally, the function would also be able to handle four projects for the year. Over time, however, due to its acceptance of projects, it completes only one or two projects. As time goes by, its completion rates fall to zero while the function continues to take on additional work. This is a perfect example of *the customer service death spiral.* By taking on more projects, the IT function assumes it is being customer friendly, but customer service will actually be lowered due to non-delivery.

It is for this reason that all IT functions must have an adequate prioritization and approval process. This process ensures that when new activities surface on the IT agenda, the process can be properly sequenced in the portfolio and other activities can either be diverted or redirected. The approval and prioritization process should involve both IT as well as business personnel. This way the lines of communications are open to both the business and IT functions, and expectations can be met effectively and realistically.

Figure 1.1. 5   Manage Client Relationship

Manage Client Relationship. The business of information technology is no different than selling watches at Wal-Mart or buying a burger from McDonalds. Clearly the emphasis should be on the customer and the customer's needs. IT functions cannot afford to be insular. As an entity the function needs to be outward focused. Internal activities related to how IT operates and how things get built and delivered all have to be taken care of, but should never be sacrificed for the customer.

The term "customers" can be broken down into many different constituents: immediate customers, second-level customers, extended customers, stakeholders, and sponsors.

Immediate Customers are those who have a direct relationship with the IT project team. These are people who work directly with the IT function and are on an equal basis on the business side to ensure that the work gets accomplished. Say the corporate division of "Beverage X" wants to develop a safety and health system. The IT system development team needs the business customers to be intricately involved with the development effort. In some companies, the immediate customers lead the development effort to make sure the job gets done.

Second-Level Customers are those who receive the impact of an activity completed by an immediate customer. For example, after the new system was delivered by the corporate IT function for Beverage X, the corporate customer makes sure it works to specification. Let's say safety and health data collection occurs in the business unit of Beverage X. Those business unit users are the second-level customers of the Safety and Health application.

Extended Customers are those who benefit from a system in the long term. At Beverage X the system was delivered and used by corporate, and data gathering occurred in the business unit. We might later determine that the ultimate beneficiary of the work being done could be a state agency that requested the safety and health information from Beverage X. They would be our extended customers.

Stakeholders are clients who might not have direct input into the project, but are impacted by its results. Let's change to a financial services example involving a project where one of the outputs was a financial report detailing ongoing capital projects within a company. The stakeholders for this project are the CEO, the CFO, and the president of a division within the company. They have input into the kind of reports being generated, but other than specifying what they would like to see, the stakeholders are completely separated from the IT process.

Sponsors are some of the most important business people on a project—if not the most important. The sponsor is the one who ultimately signs the check on the project and is the one the IT function makes sure is satisfied with its completion. Some business sponsors are deeply involved in the project and serve on some type of steering committee with the senior level IT person. In some organizations, the business sponsor gives final approval of a project's scope changes and time adjustments.

The most important point is that each IT function must and should ensure that there is adequate customer segmentation analysis performed so that the business constituents are known and understood clearly. The key to any successful business is a clear understanding of who the customers are and what they want.

Communicating information about projects varies, depending on the customer with which the CIO is interacting. There are different levels of communication that have to be maintained. There are different activities that must be shared with the various constituents. The communication plan around a project must be clear and concise, and targeted at the varying customer base.

The IT function should manage the relationship with all the different customers. At times, the CIO needs to have a presentation at the higher level and share that information with his or her peers relative to the activity of the function the current state of IT, and where the function is headed.

Managing the relationship could mean a monthly meeting with peers and business sponsors over coffee in the company cafeteria. It could mean having dinner with the business sponsor. The IT function needs to ensure that the customer really matters to them and they will spare nothing to ensure that the goods are delivered effectively.

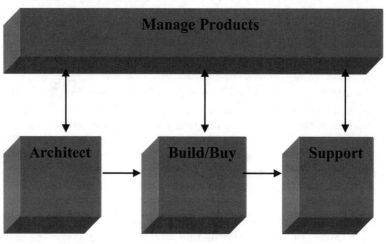

Figure 1.1. 6   Manage Products

Manage Products. There are basically two outputs from within an IT function: products and services. It is important for the IT function to view itself as a manufacturing entity that creates and delivers *"things"* to its customers. Managing that product is one of the most important aspects of the function. An example of manufactured products for the function could be the creation of reports for a maintenance system; the creation of various Intra/Internet applications developed internally; the delivery of a data warehouse for the storage of corporate information; document management system; etc.

The manufacturing of these products is done with relative ease if the unit is dependent on methodologies for the delivery of system. Methodologies are the mode, method, and way in which an IT function operates in the creation of its products.

System Development Life Cycle (SDLC), as they are called, is the language used by the IT function for the delivery of its products. The methodology varies depending on the type of product being delivered. For example, the methodologies could be for a) package software; b) custom development; c) infrastructure activities; and 4) re-engineering activities.

Package software are products bought and delivered to the end user with minimal customization or code changes. Custom-developed products are those developed internally by taking the user specification and translating them into "computerese" and then delivering an end product. The product is architect. Infrastructure activities vary quite a lot: from the purchase of new servers, new platform equipment, and hardware; to the installation of various PBX lines for communication within the corporation. Re-engineering activities are those that change the basic and fundamental operation of the business. It requires taking a fresh look at the business and determining how a re-design will benefit business operations.

In addition to the creation of various products is the manner in which the IT department services them. It is first built or bought off the shelf and then supported after delivery to the customer. This book does not focus on the fundamentals of architectonic, building, and buying. Any system development life cycle can get into the detail of those activities. The purpose of this book is to give you a high-level view of what happens in IT operations.

Some suggest the best way to manage the entire IT function is to create a project management office. This PMO would be responsible for ensuring that proper methodologies are followed, that the right tools are in place to address the needs of the IT community, and that IT operates as a clearinghouse for all information related to its operations management.

Project management offices can be central to one particular function within the business unit and have a global reach across the entire business. The rigidity of the governance model in most cases is what drives the usage and how drastic an implementation of the PMO is. There are many possibilities for a PMO. There could be a PMO at the corporate level which has global influence and reach across the entire organization. This corporate PMO would be responsible for summarizing all the information across all line of businesses. Additionally, there could be a PMO that is specific to one particular business unit or function that is responsible for governing and driving the successful implementation of projects. In most circumstances, the business unit PMO would report to the corporate level PMO.

For a company to determine whether or not it needs a PMO to manage its product, it must be able to a) sense the direction, b) craft a vision and 3) map the direction of the PMO.

Sensing the Direction (Why have a PMO?)

The Organization Needs:

- A standardized system development
- Set methodology for addressing development issues
- A coordinated way of developing projects across business units
- Have managers who manage projects in a defined coordinated manner
- A formal, structured process for assessing overlaps in project resources across the enterprise
- To standardize forms and tools to address system development

- Proper detail along with concise and accurate information related to the stages of development
- To "re-direct" or "control" the implementation of cross-business unit projects
- To show how accurately and concise an enterprise is as it relates to project development from a performance measurement standpoint

The above are some specific reasons why any business would have some kind of project management organization to manage the products and services they produce. After sensing the direction, the organization must now craft the vision.

Crafting the Vision

Crafting the vision is making certain the following functional points are covered:

- Project Management
- Business Systems Planning
- Performance Measurement

with the purpose of undertaking and effectively managing projects with a standard methodology for system development and systems planning. An additional purpose would be to accurately report to senior management the effectiveness of the IT function, not only within a business unit, but across the enterprise.

Based on the direction, the obvious action for any organization is to then pursue the activity of actually creating a *Project Management Office*.

Mapping the Direction

It is imperative that the function is properly staffed with business functional experts and administrative help to cover the areas of

- Project Management
- Business Systems Planning
- Performance Measurement.

Not only does this center become an activity within the organization, but it becomes a function with the specific charter of looking at project management, planning, and performance measurement for the overall IT function.

The case must be made that this function can be in a business unit to manage its activity and it can be at the corporate office to manage activity of the overall corporation. It all depends on the number of initiatives that the function has to undertake.

Let's take an imaginary trip to explain the overall picture of the *Project Management Office* in a corporation. First, all planning activity should be taking place within individualized business units when they have been given any kind of enterprise edict from the corporate-level leaders. Second, specific business units would be busy strategizing and determining what the varied initiatives would be for the upcoming year to address the business unit in support of the corporate strategy.

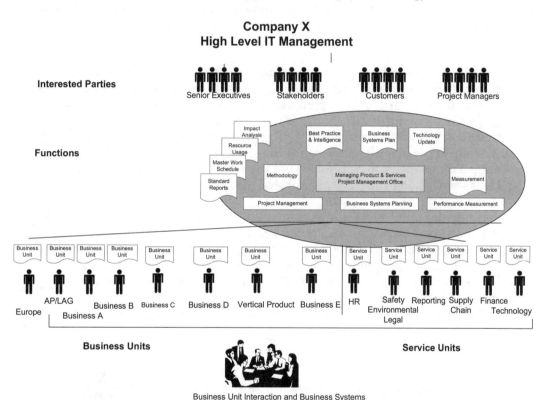

Figure 1.1. 7   High-Level IT Management

Within each business unit, depending on the number of activities that needs to be monitored and managed, there should be a PMO to manage resources, cost and people, and to ensure that projects are on schedule. The PMO is there to redirect and consolidate initiatives and to ensure that business units are performing tasks beneficial to the corporation. Before initiatives can be started, however, the PMO must drive the business unit to develop a comprehensive business systems plan that documents all the activities that should occur within the next one to three years.

It must be stated clearly that all businesses, depending on their initiatives and activities, could have a PMO within the business function and also have a PMO within the IT function. The PMO in the business is normally called the *"Program" Management Office*, which differs from the IT PMO, the *Project Management Office*.

The difference between the two is that within the business, the Program Management Office could manage programs that not only have an IT component, but also finance, human resource, or other functional component. A program could have many projects, hence the differentiation of the "program office" versus the "project office."

The corporate PMO will drive the business PMO to develop its business systems plan. The corporate PMO not only manages the business systems plan process, but also sets the standard for the appropriate methodologies that should be used throughout the company. It also manages the performance management (measurement) process for the company. The corporate PMO office is responsible for summarizing all the information from the different businesses of the corporation and presenting a comprehensive picture of what the corporation—not the individual businesses—will be doing for the upcoming one-to-three years.

Numerous individuals will have an interest in the activities of the Project Management Office. Project managers can get rolled-up information—from a resource and cost effective perspective—to help them manage their projects more effectively. Senior executives can get consolidated information from the entire enterprise in one singular location. Stakeholders, those that might be affected by the activities of individualized projects, can inquire about some of the fundamentals of a project. Customers can get up-to-date information on the status of their projects.

Manage

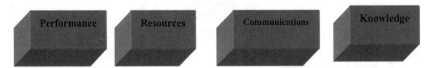

Figure 1.1. 7a.   Managing People

Manage People (Performance, Resources, Communication and Knowledge). This by far is the most important aspect of technology management. Managing technology people is quite different from managing employees such as accountants, biologists, or nurses. During the mid to late 90s—during the Internet revolution—it was common for college graduates to jump right into the Internet industry and begin receiving six figure salaries and hefty stock options. Still other firms were more than willing to double or triple their salaries. That was the 90s—a period of absolute "crazed" salaries given to individuals who were not capable of managing or helping themselves out of a trivia game.

Then again, that's just my personal resentment for not being able to earn what those graduates did. More power to them. My kids will probably one day ask me, "Daddy, where were you during the 90s? Why aren't you a multi-zillionaire?"

People, no matter what industry they are in, have basic expectations of what their workplace should be and what to expect from their employers. There is a long list of what those expectations can be. Here are some of the more common ones:

- An appreciation of the work environment

- Open and frank discussions

- Brainstorming on all activities within the group or unit

- Relaxed and comfortable atmosphere with limited stress, but if stressed, will seek effective means to manage accordingly

- An environment that operates with the mentality to manage risk

- Flexibility to make mistakes and not feel threatened by them

- Free and open communication and the sharing of knowledge

- Honest day's work for an honest day's pay

- Be judged by work accomplished rather than looks or other features

The profession doesn't matter, such expectations are basic. An organization that is able to capitalize on a free and open environment for a calculated risk and open thought will be able to survive and even prosper.

"Management" involves getting subordinates to do things that you are not able or do not care to do because of your level of responsibility. A critical component of managing people is being able to create and foster relationships. Such an atmosphere lends itself to trust. Without trust, an organization cannot survive. Without trust, an organization will not be able to move forward and accomplish its mission.

A clear focus in the workplace on relationships will not only make life better, but will improve the work environment. Author Margaret Wheatley puts it this way in her book *Leadership and the New Science*: "The learning for all of us seems clear. If power is the capacity generated by our relationships, then we need to be attending to the quality of those relationships. We would do well to ponder the realization that love is the most potent source of power."

Those responsible for managing people must be able to form tremendous bonds with them. Managers must also be able to lead the people to better themselves, and not just the organization in which they operate.

On this aspect of leadership and how one performs as a leader, Larry Bossidy of Allied Signal once said, "The answer is, how are the people you lead doing? Do they learn? Do they visit customers? Do they manage conflict? Do they initiate change? Are they growing and getting promoted? You won't remember when you retire what you did the first quarter of 1994. What you will remember is how many people you helped have a better career because of your interest and your dedication to their development. When confused as to how you're doing as a leader, find out how the people you lead are doing."

Leaders cannot afford to focus solely on the requirement of the organization. They need to also focus on their employees and building relationships. It is a tit-for-tat scenario: if the organization is focused on the employee, the employee will in turn focus on the organization. This focus naturally drives employees to focus on the company, its goals, and missions. This drives the company to its goal of marketplace success

Management needs to focus on building up employees through mentorship and other career-building exercises. There needs to be a focus on the employee's ultimate goal in life, even if it's to be a CEO, CIO or CFO. From there, the manager should be able to devise a plan with the employee as to what needs to be accomplished not only from the current assignment, but what needs to be accomplished at the current firm, in addition to future endeavors within the career path of that individual.

Product and Service Delivery. The manner in which products and services are delivered to the customer has direct correlation to the system methodology that is used. The system methodology mentioned before details the task that should be performed by the IT personnel—from the analysis phase of the project throughout the implementation period.

The implementation phase is considered a completion phase. It is a phase in which systems are completed, data is converted, users are tested, and the system is turned on for actual usage with real and live data. When a general contractor completes the construction of a new home, he turns the keys over to the new homeowner. The final walk-through with the builder has a lasting affect on the homeowner.

Figure 1.1. 7b.   Product and Service Delivery

A house could be built in masterful form and if effective "hand-holding" is not done, there could be negative feelings between the builder and homeowner. If the house is turned over in shabby form—garbage out back, unused materials in the front, or construction seems shoddy—the builder will have a customer relationship problem.

It is no different for IT. Most projects fail at the end because the "builders" of the system forget about effective user training, user documentation, and post-audit work. An example of post-audit work could be a review of deliverables that were promised at the beginning of the project. Project managers need to ensure that what was promised was actually delivered, whether it is in the measure of actual return on investment or on headcount reduction due to the new system.

1.2   The Overall Planning Environment

When it comes to the fundamentals of planning, it's a foregone conclusion that IT professionals thoroughly understand their company's business environment. They must understand the drivers of growth and success, and they must understand the information that could create paradigm shifts in their company's business operations.

Consider your home budget—the simplest form of planning that we perform on a monthly, if not daily, basis. Sometimes it's actually terrifying to sit down and figure out where all our hard-earned money went. In most cases, we can clearly state the input to our budget planning— from where the money came. But, it's quite another story analyzing the output of our money. We understand that salary, wages, investment returns, and income make up most of our input; while bills account for all of our output. The question is, which bills must be paid, which bills can wait, and what expenses can be cut or at least scaled back?

Fact is organizations are not much different from a person who balances their checkbook, or analyzes how to save for a new Porsche or their kids' college education. These are tough choices, but like the person, the organization has to understand the potential values to be gained from expenditures before committing to them. Questions must be asked as to whether investments are for short-term gains or long-term rewards.

Understanding the various processes in the organization is an important requirement before delving into planning. Processes such as enterprise planning, business plans, business systems plans, financial planning, initiative planning and budgeting must at least be understood from a conceptual standpoint before delving into the actual form and content of the business systems plan. We will look at this in an overview form and will address it more in detail when we discuss planning issues as they relate to the organization.

The following diagram indicates how most organizations begin the planning process with a call from the corporate planning arm, which usually reports to the CEO. This unit serves as the earpiece and spokesperson in terms of enterprise strategy from the CEO. Next, the information is shared with individual business units in the organization who in turn create business plans for their unit.

For example, an insurance company CEO has an overall strategy for marketing to new customers across all businesses within the organization. The healthcare, individualized insurance, reinsurance, brokerage, investment, and international arm of the corporation would prepare plans that move their individual businesses in the direction the CEO has set.

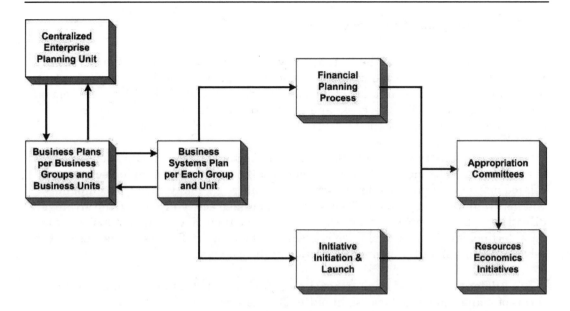

Figure 1.2. 1   Organizational Planning Process

The business plan can be crafted and created separately from the business systems plan.   The business plan serves as a roadmap for the direction the business is headed.   Once the business plan is created, the players on the system side and the business side should meet to draft the BSP.   The BSP will serve as the "IT Bible" for the technology project manager and also as a communication vehicle for the business to ensure understanding of the particular initiatives being undertaken by the IT unit.

Once both plans are completed, the resources from a financial standpoint must be galvanized via the financial planning process.   Normally various "appropriation" committees within a company have a say in how the money is spent.   Appropriation committees usually consist of senior level business, systems, and operations level personnel who must make the difficult decision as to which initiative—given the cost and the risk—should be undertaken. Once funds have been approved and allotted, development of an initiative (initiative creation) occurs next, followed by the actual launch of the project.

That was a quick high-level overview of what might happen within an organization or company as it tries to retrieve the much-needed dollars required for its projects.

1.3   IT Management and Governance

The management of the IT function varies from company to company. Ideally, IT management and governance should be determined by the design of the organization and by the direction of its leaders or board of directors. The management and manner in which IT is received and the relative importance of its function is determined not so much by the IT function, but by the needs of the business.

Your industry also drives the relative importance of the management and oversight of the IT function. Within the chemical industry, for example, technology related matters are not considered strategic in nature. In many chemical companies you may find that the primary IT person does not have active input into the strategic direction of the company. On the other hand, in the financial services industry—where data, technology and rate of change is greater—the primary IT person has a seat at the table and helps drive the strategic direction of the company.

Before we proceed any further, let's define some titles that are important in terms of management and oversight of the IT function:

Table 1.3. 1   Corporate Players

Abbreviation	Definition	Explanation
CEO	Chief Executive Officer	Primary person responsible for running the entire corporation or enterprise.
COO	Chief Operating Officer	Primary person responsible for the smooth operation of all businesses within the enterprise. This person is normally responsible for all operations as well as systems activities within the company.
CFO	Chief Financial Officer	Primary person responsible for the oversight of all financial activities within the enterprise.
CIO	Chief Information Officer	Primary person responsible for the oversight of all technology

		activities within the enterprise.
BU CEO	**Business Unit Chief Executive Officer**	Primary person responsible for the business operation of a business unit or sub-unit of the company.
BU CIO	**Business Unit Chief Information Officer**	Primary person responsible for all information activities undertaken by a particular business unit.
BFA	**Business Functional Areas**	Areas such as *Operations and Manufacturing,*
CFA	**Corporate Functional Areas**	Areas such as *Marketing, Accounting, Human Resources, Finance, Safety, Environmental*

Note that there are three standard forms of organizational structure: flat, hierarchical, and matrix. *Information Technology* at times helps drive and influence the organizational structure; however, it is the business areas that truly identify the kind of organizational structure that each firm uses.

Hierarchical Organizational Structures. This is the most common type of organization. It has an ultimate senior-level executive to whom all accountability rests. The senior-level executive has subordinates beneath him/her and those subordinates have subordinates and so on.

In many corporations, there is a senior executive who is responsible for a function or a business, such as a senior executive who is vice president of human resources. The CEO and/or chairman of the board have direct accountability for the performance of all areas of the company. In certain cases the CEO and chairman of the board are two separate people. Recently there's been a trend toward merging the responsibility of the two individuals into one. The more the positions merge together, from an audit and oversight perspective, the greater the risk in terms of governance and accountability. Since the chairman/CEO has direct accountability for the performance of these particular units, whether they are business units or corporate functional units, then the chairman/CEO normally hires senior executives who are experts in their particular field to execute the strategies.

The chairman/CEO oversees the entire organization, but in the case above we see that the company is divided along two distinct lines: 1) *corporate and functional areas*, and 2) Business Groups. In most cases, the *corporate and functional areas* have no direct revenue responsibility, which means that they do not have the responsibility for generating revenues or funds.

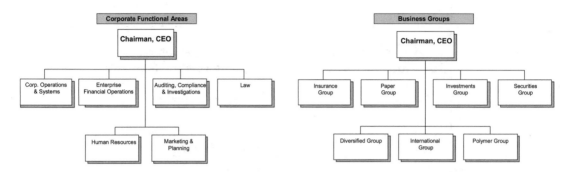

Figure 1.3. 1 Functional Areas Organizational Structure   **Figure 1.3. 2 Business Groups Organizational Structure**

The business groups, however, are normally groups or units that are the primary "bread winners" for the company. These are the units that sell products and services developed by the company. The corporate and functional areas consist of—but by no means are limited to—such functions as human resources, law, marketing and planning, financial operations, audit, control, accounting, finance, and system development.

Depending on the type of business your company is engaged in, your business units could run the gamut. The gamut could be a) a paper group responsible for developing paper products and selling it to the public; b) an investment group that invests the company's money with the hope of having high returns; c) an international group responsible for selling the company's products and services in international markets; d) a securities group that sells security instruments to the public, and e) a polymer group that markets and sells polymer paper products.

In certain instances, some companies have a chief operating officer as well as a president, or both. Depending on their oversight in the organization, there might be a need to have separate and independent roles. The larger the organization, there is a greater need for independent positions and roles. In smaller organizations these roles are collapsed and driven by one person.

Within a corporation there needs to be a system of checks and balances to ensure proper accountability. The CEO or chairman reports to the board of directors. The board of directors consists of independent members of the business community with little or no ties to the management structure. The board represents shareholders who invested in the company and serve as an oversight committee for all decisions that are made by the company.

Some boards are active while others are passive. Active boards are keenly aware and involved in the company's decision-making activities. Active board members meet quite often with senior level executives to ensure that the company is following through on the expectations of the shareholders.

Passive board members have limited involvement in decision-making and take their lead from the chairman or CEO. Recently, especially during 2002, we saw many companies experience internal control failures. This led to shareholders' suits targeted at the board of directors. These suits led to boards of directors becoming extremely active rather than remaining passive. An active board indicates active accountability to the shareholders. They also hold the CEO, chairman, and president accountable for the firm's decision-making.

From an IT standpoint, the hierarchical structure can be beneficial to the implementation of technology throughout the company. However, the position of the technology department within the hierarchy will determine its influence and its level of success. In certain cases the IT department could be a subordinate function to the finance department. In this case all decisions are made from the perspective of the financial function, which in and of itself accounts for things more on an accounting/investment basis, moreover from a strategic basis.

If the IT department heads have direct access to senior-level business decision-makers, the level of influence of technology throughout the business can be high. There is a need, therefore, in a structured hierarchy for the technology function to be near the top level of the hierarchy in order to be effective.

Flat Organizational Structure. This structure is most often found in start-up companies and those where decision-making needs to be executed rapidly. The flat organizational structure eliminates the many levels of subordinates and usually consists of a senior-level executive followed by decision-makers and then executers. There is no need for middle management. Such a structure increases the speed of decision-making, but it also renders many executives not only senior strategic leaders but also those who actually perform implementation activities. Start-up and entrepreneurial firms utilize the flat organizational structure primarily because of their limited number of employees, and also because in start-up mode the need to make quick decisions is necessary. As the organization grows and increases in size—in both employees and processes—the organization migrates from being a flat organization structure to one that is primarily hierarchical in nature.

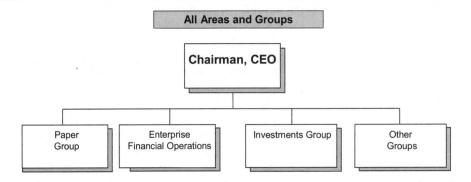

Figure 1.3. 3   All Areas and Groups Organizational Structure

In the flat structure IT activities are executed in silos, apart from the rest of the business. The knowledge level of the senior person is what drives the involvement of technology in the overall organization. The flat structure lends itself well to business functioning and execution, but could limit the ability of technology to be implemented in a holistic form. It is one-dimensional from the perspective of the company head and doesn't lend itself well to cross-pollination across businesses and functions.

Matrix Organizational Structure. This form involves one or more supervisors directing an employee. The purpose for the matrix organization is that it ensures proper accountability and it facilitates the increased cross-pollination of information technology across the entire business landscape. Within a matrix management function, it is possible to have a member in the finance department of a business unit reporting to the senior level executive in that business (president of the business) and also to have that same individual on a dotted-line (secondary) reporting relationship to the senior financial person in the corporate office (CFO of the company).

The company president and CFO complete the circle of accountability to ensure that decisions are carried out in the form that is expected.

Matrix Management ensures the following:

- Checks and Balances: Assures that all relevant personnel across organizations are involved in the initiation and review of significant initiatives.

- Accountability: Places responsibility for commitments (schedule, cost, productivity, etc.) on a specific employee, and assures that the accountable employees are identifiable and their performance measurable.

- Skill Sharing: Permits the temporary assignment of critical resources to specific activities for defined periods of time to accomplish critical activities.

- Multiple Reporting: Defines the organizational approach that permits skilled employees to report to multiple superiors whose defined responsibilities are different but whose corporate goals are consistent. Multiple reporting helps link operations and systems activities to business initiatives.

Matrix management has both friends and foes. Supporters of this form of management contend its best at ensuring that accountability is clear and executed properly across the organization. Another benefit is that it seems ideal for the implementation and roll out of information technology across the business. Still, opponents say it fails to help managers achieve their objectives and can be confusing when a manager is accountable for two or more subordinates.

The matrix organization runs best when complemented with an operations and systems organization. Let's examine it. "Operations" is part of any organization, whether it is manufacturing, insurance, or investments. Every organization has its mode, manner, and processes – also known as "operations".

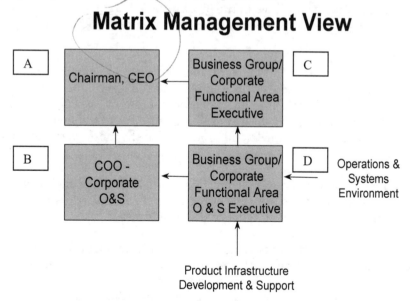

Matrix Management View

Figure 1.3. 4   Matrix Management View

Operations exist to provide information and transaction processing services to internal and external customers in an effective and efficient manner. Technology, as you know, is the systems in place along with data and processes to ensure that the business operates effectively. The system charter is to efficiently provide and maintain timely, high quality systems in conformance with business priorities and architectural standards.

In the example above of the view of matrix management, we see that chairman/CEO (A) has two entities that feed him information (B & C). The first is the chief operating officer (COO) or the head of corporate operations and systems (O&S). Second are the business groups and all the corporate functional area senior executives. The chairman and CEO can be sure that 1) operations are in place to ensure business execution and 2) business decisions are carried out effectively by the senior business and corporate executives.

Box D indicates—whether it is a financial area or a business area such as a paper product—there are operations and systems that coordinate the technology activity and the operations to ensure business continuity and execution.

View C to D is the product infrastructure and focuses on the development and deployment of product for the business. It contains the mechanism that must be in place to ensure that products are correctly developed and formulated.

In the manufacturing environment, for example, this view answers questions such as "What products do I have in the pipeline?" "Where are my salespeople?" "Are we in the proper markets?" "Are we delivering the right product to the right market in a timely fashion?"

View B to D focuses on the operations and systems components. It answers the question, "What technology do we have in place to deliver products and services in an efficient, effective manner?" In financial services, areas of coverage could answer such questions as "What technology does my sales agent have in the field?" "How can they deliver to the customer a complete end product with the most up-to-date market information?"

In a manufacturing environment this would be the key engine of supply chain functions where all activities from the purchasing of raw materials to the creation of product development to product delivery will be addressed.

If we take the picture above and orientate it into a triangular form, we can delve deeper into the activities of the organization that have the matrix form structure. This orientation can be seen on the next page. As previously mentioned, the CEO has two sources of information: 1) from the corporate operations and systems executive which could be the chief operating officer; and, 2) from the business group/corporate functional area (BG/CFA Executive). The levels beneath that include the CIO who now reports to the chief operating officer/corporate operation and systems executive. The CIO in this case has a corporate department which we will explore later.

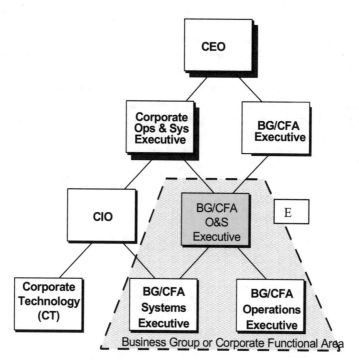

Figure 1.3. 5   Matrix Form Structure

Area E is considered the business environment where product infrastructure is deployed for the development of product and wherein an efficient operations and systems environment is orchestrated to maintain business development, continuity, and optimal information flow. It is important to note that in some large organizations there exists a corporate technology department that supports the COO, but also drives such functions as research and development, architecture, and technology planning. This is our next topic of discussion.

The matrix management works best because of its coverage of the areas of checks and balances, accountability, multiple reporting, and effective sharing across the organizational landscape. The other structures, though offering their positive and negatives, carry with them the potential of a higher level of risk.

It must be noted that there is a fourth type of organizational structure that has taken form in the past few years. It is called the *Networked Organization*, which is information dependent. Networked organizations utilize information and communication systems to help with the information and communication flow evident in large organizations.

Due to the myriad of information dynamics and sharing, this type of organization seems flat and also hierarchical at the same time. Advocates of this structure say it focuses on creativity, but eliminates bureaucratic norms consistent with hierarchical structure. The information decision-making is driven by large and massive amounts of data storage in data warehouses and is parsed via data mining, data visualization, and other creative analysis tools. This structure is still somewhat under development and therefore futuristic.

1.4   Role of the Chief Information Officer

The chief information officer (CIO) is no different from a CEO in terms of his/her function in a large organization. The CIO, like that of the CEO, oversees the entire organization in terms of technology development and deployment—not in terms of business development.

Chief information officers have relationships with 1) their internal organization – corporate technology; 2) business groups, which consists of business executives; and 3) corporate functions, which consists of corporate functional activities. In this role the CIO serves to:

- Unite the IT community and foster innovation;
- Extend horizontal integration and mobility;
- Ensure that all cohesive technology direction is driven throughout the organization.

In the role detailed above, the CIO works with the head of each business to ensure

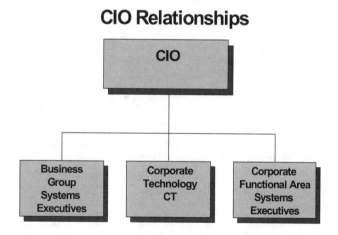

Figure 1.4. 1   CIO Relationships

the effective alignment of technology strategy and business strategy. This is driven by meetings with various senior leaders from the major functions of the organization. The CIO is accountable for:

- Oversight of information technology both within lines of business, across corporate functional areas, and throughout the entire organization

- Implementing effective IT application throughout the organization.

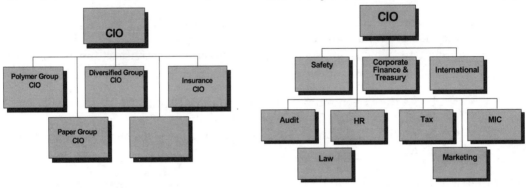

Figure 1.4. 2   CIO Business Group Relationships   Figure 1.4. 3 CIO Corporate Function Relationships

In many large organizations there may be a CIO for each of the businesses and functional areas. This is dependent on the size of the organization. The example above has a corporate CIO, but within every function of the business, whether it is the polymer, diversified, paper or insurance group, there is another CIO.

In smaller organizations those titles change to something like "director" or "manager of technology." In other organizations, unlike the one above, corporate functional areas are grouped together. It is not uncommon that the areas of Corporate Finance Treasury Tax and Audit, has one senior-level IT personnel due to the consistency of information, need, and usage.

As mentioned earlier, CIO's normally have a support unit that helps them set the standard for the development of technology throughout the organization. This group serves as the CIO's brain trust, and they are responsible for driving the directives of the CIO throughout the organization. The example listed below is not all-encompassing, but serves a general framework for the types of activities covered by this group.

CIO Corporate Information Technology Relationship

Figure 1.4. 4   CIO Corporate Information Technology Relationship

The corporate IT group normally is responsible for a) setting policies, b) setting standards, c) setting architectural guidelines, and d) building the IT community within the entire organization. This group is developed under the direction of the CIO and is tasked with ensuring IT organizational effectiveness. Such responsibilities are further defined by:

> ***Set Policies.*** Policies are set by working with business groups and corporate functional areas system executives.

- Define policies;
- Define roles and responsibilities;
- Define accountabilities;
- Define frameworks;
- Aid the Systems Executives in communicating policies to their IT community;
- Monitor the use of policies.

> ***Set Standards:*** Standards are developed by researching new and emerging technologies and processes and defining clearly how they can benefit the organization.

- Research emerging technologies and processes;
- Coordinate the working groups that will define standards, including:
  - Rationale

- Guidelines
- Examples
- Products;
- Create shared services when appropriate (e.g., groupware, Internet, LAN/WAN Admin., etc.);
- Aid Systems Executives in communicating the standards to their IT community;
- Monitor the use of standards.

Set Architectural Guidelines: Architecture is the framework that consistent data, technology, and processes are built on.

- Set architectural guidelines for:
  - Corporate IT Architecture
  - Corporate Technology Architecture
  - Business Group IT Architecture;
- Aid the systems executives in communicating architectural guidelines to their IT community;
- Monitor the use of architectural guidelines.

Build the IT community: Every community needs a vision, goals, and objectives and a shared sense of the direction in which the organization is headed. Information technology is no different. Policies and procedures need to be in place to ensure everyone is headed in the same direction.

- Create centers of excellence/competence;
- Standardize organizational structures;
- Create HR policies and processes for the IT community;
- Standardize reward and recognition;
- Standardize training and development of IT community;
- Extend horizontal integration and mobility;
- Communication;
- Sharing of ideas, problems, and skills across business groups and geography (e.g., technology information forums, group events, groupware for idea sharing, problems experienced).

In addition, there are different areas that assist CIOs in achieving their goals:

Corporate Architecture and Administration

The architecture function defines and articulates IT architecture in five areas: application, communications, data, platform, and security. The goal is to provide guidance to the IT community in the selection of business group technical architectures that allow interchangeability, and connect systems and components.

This function also focuses on architecture at the enterprise and business unit level for application, communication, data, platform, and security. Key activities for this function are:

- Corporate Technology Policy
- Enterprise Standards
- System Approval Process & Support
- Business Systems Planning
- Information Technology Metrics
- Information Technology Budget Oversight & Coordination.

Emerging Technologies

The emerging technology group conducts or oversees all IT research within the company on behalf of the CIO. The function identifies and evaluates promising emerging technologies, and works closely with business and corporate functional areas to ensure the successful implementation of these technologies in support of critical business initiatives. Key activities of this function are:

- Technology Research & Development
- Testing Lab for BGs and CFAs
- Information Technology Library
- Usability Lab
- Applied Research
- Technology Transfer
- Technology Forecast
- People Pollination
- Imprimatur on New/Requested Technology.

Communication Deployment

This function is normally responsible for promoting the effective use of groupware, Internet, and Intranet technology throughout the corporation. It works with the business groups and support organizations to establish the appropriate technical environments, recommend standards and guidelines, coordinate the sharing of information, and interface with key vendors.

2   *Understanding the Business before IT*

Before we delve into the activities of IT planning, we should focus on the various aspects of business planning. For purposes of this text, "business planning" refers to the whole process of strategy development, various authorizations, and implementation and monitoring activities that exist in an organization.

Of course, we know that the primary purpose of the IT function is to enable the organization to reach and evaluate initiatives within its business units. Lack of formality indicates goals. So it is necessary to not only flow forward into the activities of technology management, but also to take a step back and evaluate the various processes that exist in the organization's business units. These processes, whether they are formal or informal, will give the IT function a good idea as to the ease or difficulty in implementing new technology.

The formality of the business planning process gives indication as to an organization's ability to measure. Lack of clear ability to measure indicates unclear means of structuring common processes across an organization's business landscape. Lack of ability to structure common processes; leads to a business unit's autonomy which can lead to a general failure in cost control.

I am not suggesting that there should be no business unit autonomy. I believe that there should be autonomy, but with processes in place across the organization that eliminate redundancy and counteract the effect of out-of-control initiatives.

The implementation of an organization's planning process and structured strategy development exists to:

- Identify opportunities to reduce overlap while sharing approaches and technology;
- Ensure that there is alignment of initiatives with the business drivers at the business unit level as well as at the corporate level;
- Target budgets for initiatives at the enterprise, as well as business unit level, to ensure that they have the highest value-added impact;
- Ensure there are rigid cost controls in place that won't adversely affect business goals.

Before going into further discussions, let's take a look at the big picture:

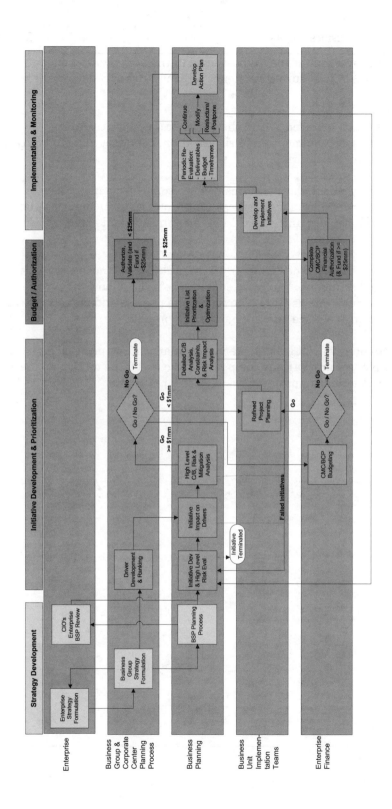

Figure 2. 1   Organizational Planning Process

47

The diagram[1] shows that at the highest level in the organization major processes should be in place to ensure consistency with the strategy development and planning processes.

The major activities involved are on the horizontal plain: a) strategy development, b) initiative development and prioritization, c) budget and authorization, and d) implementation and monitoring.

Activities on the vertical plain are areas where some of the major activities might take place: a) enterprise level, b) business unit/group level, c) business planning level, d) associated with business unit specific implementation, and e) enterprise finance level.

Let's say you are the CEO of a company with multiple business units in a conventionally managed company. You're faced with the issue of how to manage across various business units. Your role as CEO is to follow the process and make sure that all checks and balances are in place and are part of the process.

In the next chapter we will look at the various parts of the process. As we break down the overall big picture into various components, we will focus on the business activities and give peripheral attention to possible IT implications.

3   The Phases of The Business Process

3. 1   Phase 1: Strategy Development

The strategy development phase[1] is the initial phase of business development. This is where the actual business and operational planning is filtered and also where strategic initiatives for the organization are identified. The filtering is executed across multiple business levels. This serves to ensure that there is strategic alignment not only at the enterprise level, but within business units and across the IT landscape.

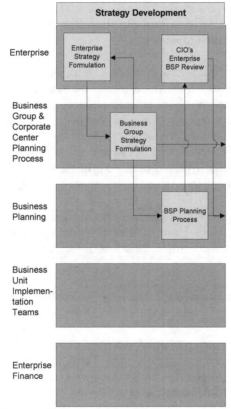

Figure 3.1. 1   Strategy Development Phase

Business unit strategy—also known as enterprise strategy—is the plan that integrates an organization's goals, policies, and action sequences into a cohesive whole. Such a strategy should identify the overall direction and intent of the organization in terms of the major drivers that are, or will be in place, to ensure business continuity.

The enterprise level is the area of the organization that is considered corporate, or where the centralized functions across the organization are developed.

The business group and corporate center planning process are those areas of the organization where specific business activities take place such as the paper group that develops paper products or the human resources function that focuses on personnel issues.

Business planning is the area of business development that focuses on the planning activities for a function. It is important to note that the planning activity could be orchestrated at the corporate level and can then flow down to the business unit level for further analysis and development.

Business unit implementation teams focus on the implementation of the initiatives extracted from the strategy that was developed either at the enterprise level or the business unit level. The implementation team ensures that the initiatives are executed based on the formulated processes of the business groups.

Enterprise finance is a key component to the overall phases of the business process because enterprise finance is involved in the authorization or distribution of financial instruments to the business to enable the business to execute its strategies.

There are huge benefits to having a properly orchestrated strategy development process across the various businesses and corporate functions of an organization. Most importantly, it eliminates the potential missteps in direction of the overall organization.

More specifically to the IT function, a well-executed strategy development shows these benefits:

- Ensures efforts are aligned with the business strategy, both within and across business groups and corporate functions;
- Identifies opportunities to leverage resources and technology;
- Minimizes redundancy.

> ***What Happens in Practice:*** *Assume that you are the CEO of a corporation where you are currently in the strategy development phase. You and your senior leadership are crafting the initiatives. You meet with the senior executive of each business unit to determine what critical initiatives need to be developed and deployed to ensure business continuity. These initiatives will counteract any possible competitive pressures in your industry. Key issues addressed could be: What are our competitors doing? What markets do we enter? How do we implement technologies to make it easier for our customers to use our products? How can we lower costs?*

3. 2   Phase 2: Initiative Development and Prioritization

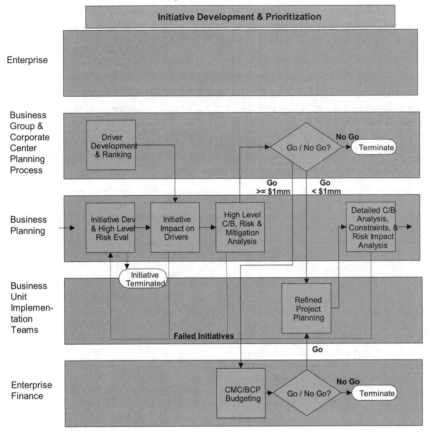

Figure 3.2.1   Initiative Development and Prioritization Phase

The development of strategies leads[2] to the development of initiatives.
Initiatives are programs or actions for upcoming business cycles. It is during this
phase that initiatives are identified and prioritized against business drivers, with
analytical integration of various factors and constraints (cost, benefit, risk assessment /
impact / mitigation, budgetary issues, etc.).

Within any organization there is a fixed amount of capital. Consider your
home and your job. At the end of your work cycle, you receive a certain amount of
money. Your job does not give you all the money you need. Some jobs afford that, but
for all intensive purposes, the job gives you a fixed amount of funds. Funds are used to
pay your mortgage, rent and, other necessities. An organization is no different.

It is during this stage that the organization compares its strategies with its amount of initiatives and with its projection of available funds. The boundary of spending is limited by the amount of funds that will be available.

There are benefits to be gained from having a structured and fundamental initiative development and prioritization process to the IT function. These benefits are:

- Leverage resources for maximum value by identifying those initiatives with the greatest value to the organization;
- Utilize a common approach and discipline for evaluating initiatives.

What Happens in Practice: *Each business unit executive and leadership team member knows that there is a fixed amount of funds. During this phase initiatives are developed without focus on financial constraints. It is possible that strategy sessions are held with key leaders in each business unit to determine the possible futures that could exist. Futures are analyzed against potential financial returns to determine the business unit continuity and to determine if going concern is a problem for the unit. Based on the analysis of potential funds, the prioritization process is enacted to either eliminate low-value initiatives or to delay certain initiatives that might be a benefit to the organization, but cannot be developed due to a constraint on available funds.*

3. 3   Phase 3: Budget and Authorization

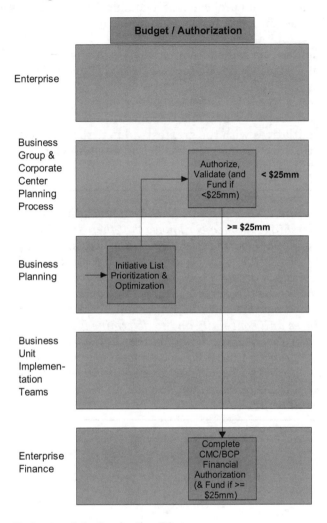

Figure 3.3. 1   Budget and Authorization Phase

The *Budget and Authorization Phase[3]* also known as the *"Bureaucratic Phase"*, is the phase where budgets are developed and orchestrated between and among various departments to ensure that key constraints are met.   The main activity of this phase is that initiatives are optimized against key decision-making factors and ultimately selected and authorized for funding. Also, specific monitoring criteria are identified with respect to budget, timeframes, deliverables, and expected benefits.

The budgeting process normally involves paperwork that gives justification to the proposed initiatives. It involves documentation of the initiatives, any potential risk, potential funds, and benefits to be gained. In addition, the time frames of the initiative from analysis to deployment, potential return, and best- and worst-case scenarios.

The benefits to be gained by the IT function are:

- Focus on the "right" efforts;
- Flexibility to add or delete analytical constraints based on changing business requirements and market influences;
- Establishment of key measures for monitoring implementation efforts.

> **What Happens in Practice:** *Following the prioritization of all potential initiatives, key implementers and project managers are asked to develop documentation that justifies the need for the initiatives. This is done at the business unit and corporate function level. Each unit is asked that for each potential initiative that there is a clear, documented, and analyzed reason to justify at the corporate level why should funds be allocated for the initiative? Some initiatives are done to generate cash, while others are done for regulatory reasons. And still others are done for maintenance reasons. These reasons are documented and serve as the springboard for the eventual launch of the initiative. This does not mean that the initiative is approved. It means the documentation is done, but following documentation, in most organizations, there are oversight boards that meet to compare initiatives to see which generates the optimum return for the organization. Authorization and approvals are sometimes done through capital management committees or done based on the authorization given to leaders within the organization. In addition, the issue of signature authorization and spending limit is usually addressed here.*

3. 4   Phase 4: Implementation and Monitoring

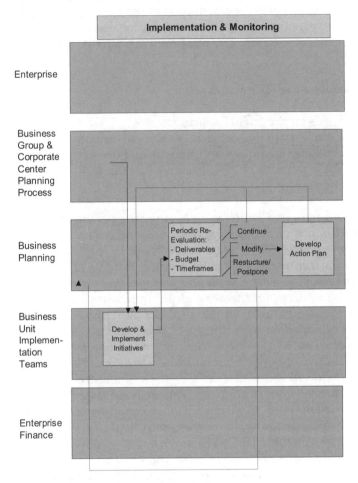

Figure 3.4. 1   Implementation and Monitoring Phase

The *Implementation and Monitoring Phase[4]* involves the launching of products or services to support the organization's direction and strategy. Following the launch, initiatives are reassessed periodically to ensure a successful implementation and that there is alignment with the business strategy and the budget, resources, and timing constraints.

Continuous evaluation of the initiative's effectiveness is accomplished during this stage. The evaluation ensures that the initiative is delivering expected results documented in the budget and authorization phase and communicated during the strategy development phase.

The benefits to the IT function for this phase are that it:

- Provides a framework for monitoring progress on initiatives;
- Ensures continual alignment of initiatives to business strategy;
- Detects early warning signs for potential failure of initiatives;
- Assesses impact of changes in the environment and the potential direction change that needs to be implemented to ensure continued success.

> ***What Happens in Practice:*** *This is the implementation stage and post-evaluation phase. During this phase, resources necessary for the creation and launch of a business initiative are obtained. In most cases, the implementation and post implementation phases are weak. This is because at the time of budgeting or development, the criterion of measurement was developed, but by the post-implementation phase, most people have moved onto new initiatives. In most cases the benefits that were promised at the strategy development phase are not tracked. An effective post-implementation evaluation process should be in place to ensure that promised deliverables are garnered. If not garnered, effective measures should be in place to either scale back on the continued roll out of the initiative or eventually stop the initiative. The actual roll out of a business initiative could yield immediate results for the business. In some cases it might take years for a return to be yielded.*

4 The Methodology of Business Planning Phases

4. 1   Strategy Development

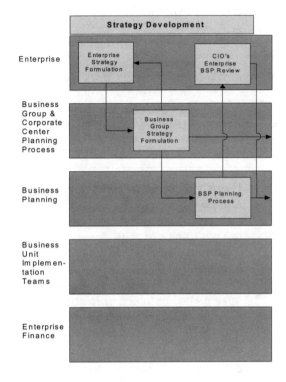

Figure 4.1. 1   Strategy Development

We will now examine each phase in detail to gain a better understanding of the various components of the overall big picture.

Strategy Development

The primary objective of the *Strategy Development Phase* is to define and clarify the organization's strategy in terms of business drivers. Specifically, this phase is where business and operational planning is filtered across multiple business levels, by management, to ensure strategic alignment among all of them.

We will evaluate each detailed box to determine the purpose of that activity, the owner, input, process, deliverable and tools used to gather the information necessary for its execution.

Enterprise Strategy Formulation

Purpose:	To ensure the enterprise has a clear overall strategy so business and corporate areas are focused on achieving the "right" goals.
Owner:	*Enterprise Planning Unit*—is normally a central unit responsible for the overall orchestration and planning at the enterprise level. This unit usually requires strategies from the various business units and corporate functional areas. These strategies and initiatives are then summarized at the executive level for the CIO and senior leadership.
Input:	Market conditions and forecasts.
Process:	Evaluate market positioning; evaluate market requirements and internal capabilities; obtain input from business groups and corporate functional areas, and define overall enterprise strategy.
Deliverable:	Enterprise strategy and drivers.
Tools / Framework:	Determined by the organization.

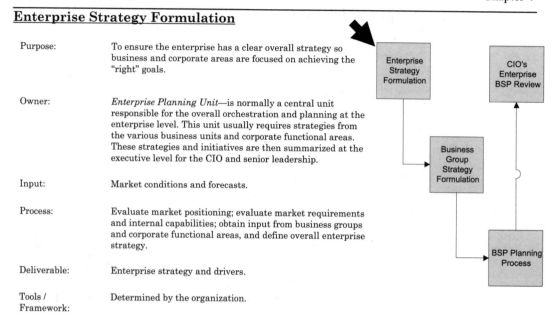

Figure 4.1. 2   Enterprise Strategy Formulation

Business Group Strategy Formulation

Purpose:	To ensure the business is both aligned with the enterprise and focused on how to best achieve its own goals and objectives.
Owner:	*Business Groups*; *Corporate Functional Areas*.
Input:	Enterprise strategy and drivers, business conditions.
Process:	<ul><li>Evaluate market requirements and internal capabilities</li><li>Discuss expectations of the *Business Group* as they relate to the enterprise</li><li>Determine appropriate strategies for each customer segment and product</li><li>Complete *Business Group Strategy* templates</li></ul>
Deliverable:	Business group strategy and drivers; Outlines for potential Initiatives
Tools / Framework:	Enterprise Planning Unit templates.

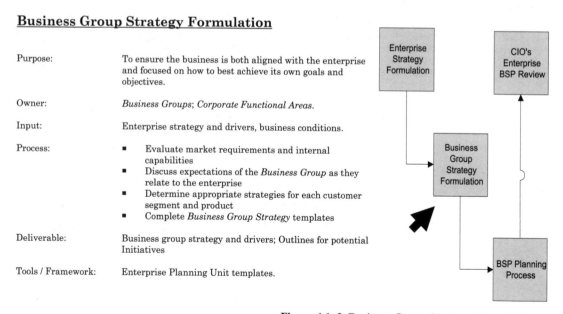

Figure 4.1. 3 Business Group Strategy Formulation

Business Systems Planning Process

Purpose: Develop operations and systems response to business
                    needs and strategies.

Owner: *CIO, Business Systems Planning Office, Business Groups,*
                    Corporate Functional Areas

Input: Business group strategy and drivers;
                    CIO (IT) strategy and drivers.

Process: ▪ Define business needs and appropriate responses;
                       formulate high-level initiatives;
                    ▪ Develop a Business Systems Plan;
                    ▪ Evaluate business group strategy and drivers.

Deliverable: High-level initiatives and systems agenda – Business
                    Systems Plan.

Tools / Framework: Business systems planning process templates.

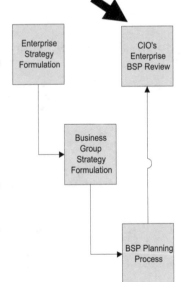

Figure 4.1. 4   Business Systems Planning Process

CIO's Enterprise BSP Review

Purpose: To identify cross-business initiatives or strategic activities
                    requiring corporate funding. To identify opportunities to
                    reduce overlap and share approaches and technology for
                    funding.

Owner: CIO

Input: *Business Systems Plans* from each business group and
                    corporate functional area.

Process: ▪ Identify overlapping initiatives;
                    ▪ Identify "out list" and strategic programs that might
                       be funded by *Corporate Information Technology*
                       Group.

Deliverable: Corporate information technology and enterprise-wide
                    initiatives list.

Tools / Framework: Corporate business systems plan process.

Figure 4.1. 5 CIO's Enterprise BSP Review

4. 2   *Initiative Development and Prioritization*

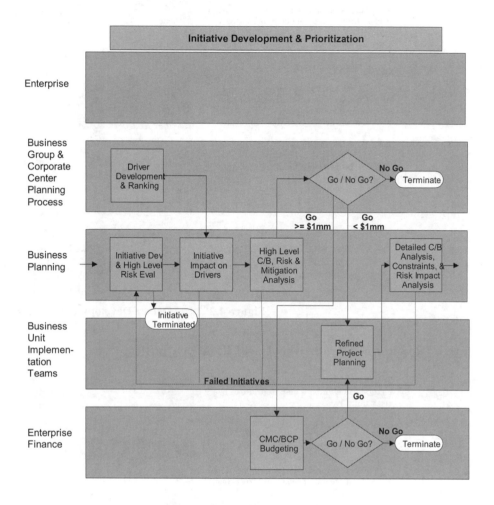

Figure 4.2. 1   Initiative Development and Prioritization

Initiative Development and Prioritization

The *Initiative Development Phase* focuses on prioritization of drivers and initiatives with analytical integration of various factors and constraints. Factors include risk assessment and impact, overall initiative benefits, and impact on business drivers. Constraints include risk mitigation costs and budgetary issues.

Driver Development and Ranking

Purpose: To refine, rank, and validate the key business drivers that reflect the business strategy.

Owner: Business Group CEO or president.

Input: List of business drivers.

Process:
- Define and validate drivers;
- Conduct a driver-to-driver pair wise comparison analysis;
- Discuss driver prioritization results.

Deliverable: Prioritized list of drivers.

Tools / Framework: This will be developed by the organization.

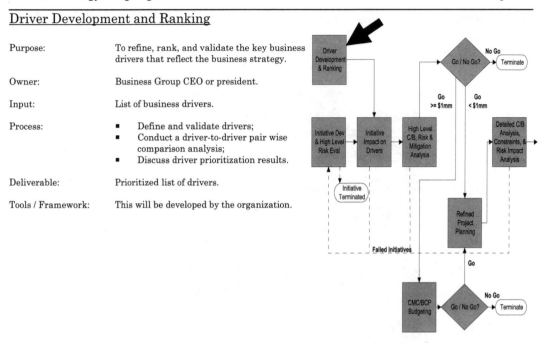

Figure 4.2. 2   Driver Development and Ranking

Initiative Development and High-Level Risk Evaluation

Purpose: To define initiatives, evaluate high-level risk factors, and eliminate inappropriate or overly risky initiatives.

Owner: Business Group Planning area.

Input: List of Initiatives.

Process:
- Examine initiatives for appropriateness;
- eliminate out-of-scope initiatives (e.g., mandates, maintenance);
- Conduct preliminary risk assessment; mitigate high-risk factors, and possibly eliminate initiatives (e.g., no sponsor).

Deliverable: Refined list of initiatives.

Tools / Framework: Business case templates.

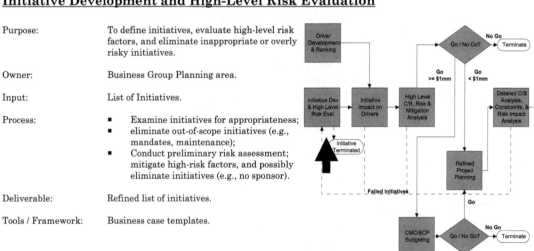

Figure 4.2. 3 Initiative Development and High-Level Risk Evaluation

Initiative Impact on Drivers

Purpose: To gauge the relative impact of initiatives on business drivers and rank the initiatives.

Owner: *Business Group Planning* area.

Input: Prioritized list of drivers and refined list of initiatives.

Process: Conduct a driver-to-initiative pair-wise ranking analysis; discuss prioritization results; and eliminate low or no impact initiatives.

Deliverable: Prioritized list of initiatives with diver impact ranking.

Tools / Framework: Driver analysis.

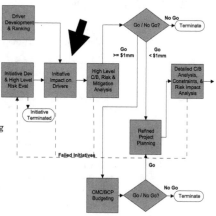

Figure 4.2. 4 Initiative Impact on Drivers

High-Level Cost /Benefit, Risk and Mitigation Analysis

Purpose: To understand the costs/benefits (C/B) and risk aspects of proposed initiatives. To create a common framework for eliminating or restructuring those that fail to meet criteria.

Owner: *Business Group Planning* area.

Input: List of initiatives.

Process: ■ Determine what is included in costs/ benefits; determine acceptable costs/ benefits parameters. Eliminate initiatives that fall outside the parameters; conduct cost vs. driver + benefit impact analyses;
                   ■ Conduct a detailed risk analysis for each initiative to determine the probability of success for meeting a) the schedule, b) the budget and c) the deliverables;
                   ■ Achieving the specified benefits; determine what mitigation plans can be made to offset high-risk projects; include revised costs/benefits impact; eliminate high risk initiatives where sufficient mitigation cannot be achieved.

Deliverable: Prioritized initiatives including costs/benefits, and risk mitigation.

Tools / Framework: Decision model.

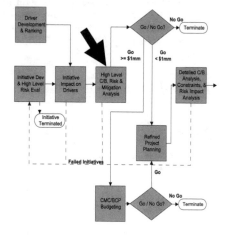

Figure 4.2. 5 High-Level Cost/Benefit, Risk and Migration Analysis

63

Managed Cost Budgeting

Purpose: To ensure consistent initiative information is
                      available for making funding decisions.

Owner: *Business Financial Management / Enterprise
                      Finance*

Input: Enterprise, Business & BSP strategic
                      information; initiative data.

Process: - Collect and validate key costs/benefits
                        information for each initiative;
                      - Ensure strategic and risk information is
                        consistent;
                      - Make "Go/No-Go" decisions based on
                        budget criteria.

Deliverable: Initiatives with appropriate financial
                      information for decision making.

Tools / Framework: Budgeting templates.

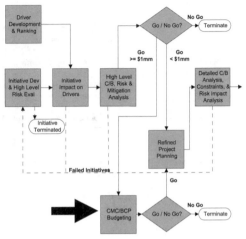

Figure 4.2. 6 Managed Cost Budgeting

Within the enterprise, once there is determination as to the level of risk that can be
absorbed, the next step is to ensure that the risk-adjusted costs are captured. These
budget numbers are captured in what is termed the *Capital Managed Cost / Budgeting
Capital Process* (CMC/BCP).

Refined Project Planning

Purpose: To enhance initiative data so a more detailed
                      analysis and prioritization can be conducted.

Owner: Business Group Planning area

Input: Detailed operational and financial information
                      for each initiative (e.g., time frames,
                      dependencies).

Process: Follow existing in-place planning processes to
                      collect data—include project manager and key
                      users.

Deliverable: Project plan for each initiative.

Tools / Framework: Project planning tools as appropriate.

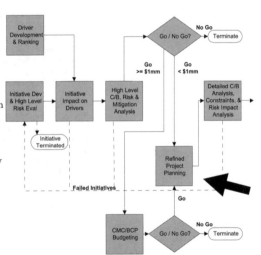

Figure 4.2. 7 Refined Project Planning

Detailed Cost/Benefit Analysis, Constraints, and Risk Impact Analysis

Purpose: To rank initiatives using updated information
                      and to analyze risk impact.

Owner: *Business Group Planning* area.

Input: Cost of risk mitigation, refined costs and
                      benefits for each initiative.

Process: ▪ Re-prioritize initiatives based on updated
                        costs;
                      ▪ Conduct risk impact analysis to refine
                        P(robability) of S(uccess) along budget,
                        schedule, deliverables, and benefits
                        dimensions;
                      ▪ Eliminate low-ranked initiatives.

Deliverable: Initiatives with updated costs/benefits and
                      probability of success.

Tools / Framework: *Decision Support Systems* or models.

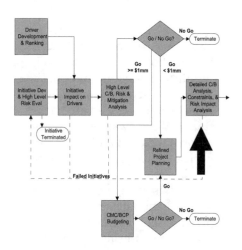

Figure 4.2. 8 Detailed Cost/Benefit Analysis, Constraints, and Risk Impact Analysis

4. 3   *Budget / Authorization*

The *Budget /Authorization Phase* encompass the final analysis and information-gathering phase in preparation for authorizing and funding the initiatives. After successfully completing the initial prioritization as well as the risk and financial reviews, the initiatives are ranked by prioritization and optimization. All decision-making factors are incorporated.

Based on results, initiatives are selected and authorized for funding from managerial and financial perspectives. Specific monitoring criteria concerning budget, time frames, deliverables, and expected benefits are established for each initiative. Once an initiative passes through this phase, it is ready for development, implementation and monitoring.

In the example above, the amount of $25 million is a threshold example and by no means is an edict for what the amount of spending must be on a certain initiative. *Signature Authorization* determines where an organization sets their threshold level for budgets. In the description to follow the $25 million could be represented as "X." X would be the threshold level at which the business group makes a determination to move an initiative forward on its own, but if it exceeds X, the initiative would have to be approved at the enterprise level.

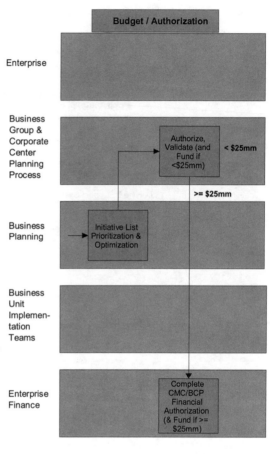

Figure 4.3.1 Budget/Authorization Phase

Initiative List Prioritization and Optimization

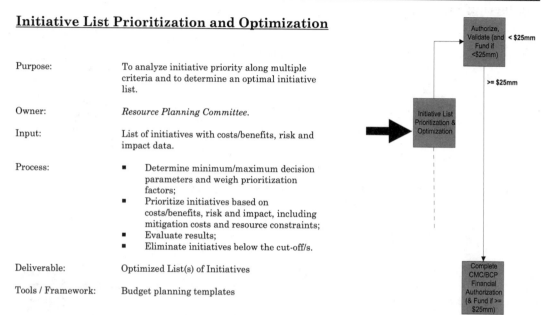

Purpose: To analyze initiative priority along multiple
                    criteria and to determine an optimal initiative
                    list.

Owner: *Resource Planning Committee.*

Input: List of initiatives with costs/benefits, risk and
                    impact data.

Process: ▪ Determine minimum/maximum decision
                      parameters and weigh prioritization
                      factors;
                    ▪ Prioritize initiatives based on
                      costs/benefits, risk and impact, including
                      mitigation costs and resource constraints;
                    ▪ Evaluate results;
                    ▪ Eliminate initiatives below the cut-off/s.

Deliverable: Optimized List(s) of Initiatives

Tools / Framework: Budget planning templates

Figure 4.3.2 Initiative List Prioritization and Optimization

Authorize, Validate, and Fund

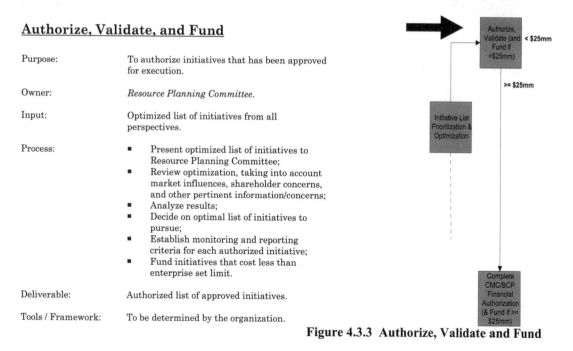

Purpose: To authorize initiatives that has been approved
                    for execution.

Owner: *Resource Planning Committee.*

Input: Optimized list of initiatives from all
                    perspectives.

Process: ▪ Present optimized list of initiatives to
                      Resource Planning Committee;
                    ▪ Review optimization, taking into account
                      market influences, shareholder concerns,
                      and other pertinent information/concerns;
                    ▪ Analyze results;
                    ▪ Decide on optimal list of initiatives to
                      pursue;
                    ▪ Establish monitoring and reporting
                      criteria for each authorized initiative;
                    ▪ Fund initiatives that cost less than
                      enterprise set limit.

Deliverable: Authorized list of approved initiatives.

Tools / Framework: To be determined by the organization.

Figure 4.3.3 Authorize, Validate and Fund

Budgeting Process

Purpose: To ensure initiative adherence to authorization guidelines for budget process.

Owner: Enterprise finance.

Input: Approved initiatives over company set amount.

Process:
- Review initiative and decision criteria to ensure adherence to initiative approval guidelines;
- Fund initiative if it meets approval guide.

Deliverable: List of Funded Initiatives over company set amount Budget templates.

Tools / Framework: To be determined by the organization.

Figure 4.3.4 Budgeting Process

4. 4   *Implementation and Monitoring*

The *Implementation and Monitoring* Phase is the final phase of the planning and prioritization process. Once the initiatives have been implemented, they must be periodically reviewed to ensure compliance with budgetary, resource, and timing constraints. If an initiative fails in this phase, one of three options may occur: modify, re-structure, or postpone the initiative. Action plans must continually be maintained to ensure successful implementation of each initiative.

The chart to the left illustrates how once approval of all initiatives has been completed and the activities have gone through the rigorous analysis and budget justification tasks, the initiative implementation is carried out by the business unit/group or corporate functional area.

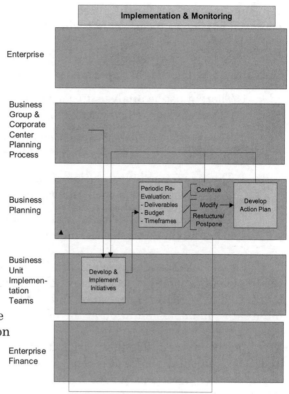

Figure 4.4.1 Implementation and Monitoring

Let's use the example of a financial services giant who has an insurance business unit. The insurance business unit has numerous agents who sell life insurance and other financial offerings. It is important for the agent to make sure they have accurate, up-to-date information so they can deliver real-time information to their clients.

The business-level executive instructs his/her subordinates that there is a need to have personal digital assistants (PDAs) in the hand of the agents. The PDAs need to be linked to a corporate database that houses vital information for the agents. There are two possible initiatives involved: 1) a business initiative to gather all the resources and potentially hire more and new sales agent in preparation for the launch of PDAs to the agent, and 2) a technology initiative to purchase PDAs, implement a data warehouse to house all the information, and make sure that all the interfaces from the field to the home office are possible.

Before implementation, there needs to be an articulated business plan as well as technology process for the successful roll out of technology and the change in potential business processes that will be derived from the PDAs.

There are many details of such an implementation phase that must be executed. Here are a few in order of importance:

1) There must be analysis to verify that the results from the strategy development phase will be yielded once the initiative is launched.

2) There must be the galvanization of resources—in both the technical and business areas—to ensure that the initiative is effectively staffed for success.

3) There must be investigation of the potential risk and associated mitigation for potential problems with undertaking such an initiative.

4) There must be determination if other organizations in the marketplace are utilizing the same or alternate technology to accomplish the same task.

Please note that the implementation phase outlines above is quite different from the implementation for a technology undertaking. *The System Development Life Cycle* mentioned in Section 1.1 describes how implementation from a systems perspective is different from implementation at the business level.

On the systems side there are four stages: 1) analysis, 2) design, 3) construction, and 4) implementation. In this sense implementation means the actual roll out or deployment of a system after its analysis, design, and construction has been completed. We can contrast that with implementation on the business environment. The difference is that from a business perspective, strategy development, initiative development, and budgeting actually precede the actual implementation of an initiative.

In the example above, it is during the implementation of a business initiative that the actual beginning process of a technology system development life cycle task begins to take place. This will be explained in Section 6. The implementation process involves the capture of resources necessary for the launch on an initiative.

Develop and Implement Initiatives

Purpose: To work toward the completion of the approved initiative.

Owner: *Business Groups and/or Systems.*

Input: Approved, validated, and funded initiative plan.

Process:
- Communicate results to the appropriate business units;
- Set up and perform detailed project planning and tracking;
- Design, develop, and code applications or other deliverables;
- Test and install systems or other initiative-related deliverables;
- Conduct user acceptant or operational workflow testing.

Deliverable: Activities aimed at successful completion of each initiative.

Tools / Framework: To be determined by the organization

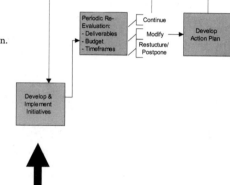

Figure 4.4.2 Develop and Implement Initiatives

Periodic Re-evaluation

Purpose: To ensure that crucial properties /performance characteristics of the initiatives have not declined.

Owner: *Business Group Program Management Office*

Input: Data for each initiative regarding status of deliverables, budget, and time frames.

Process:
- Collect crucial initiative data to assess P(robability) of S(uccess) with respect to: budget, schedule, deliverables, and benefits;
- Evaluate data for deterioration in initiative performance;
- Provide recommendations for initiative continuation, modification, or restructuring;
- Flag and forward problems for Management evaluation.

Deliverable: Activities aimed at successful completion of each initiative.

Tools / Framework: To be determined by the organization

Figure 4.4.3 Periodic Re-evaluation

Develop Action Plan

Purpose: To create/modify action plans to correct "red flags."

Owner: *Business Group Program Management Office.*

Input: Management *"Red Flag"* reports;
                      Current Initiative status and plan.

Process:
- Determine alternative solutions and choose the most feasible alternative;
- Create action plan to adjust implementation /installation process.

Deliverable: Action Plan.

Tools / Framework: Software suite of products and project planning tools.

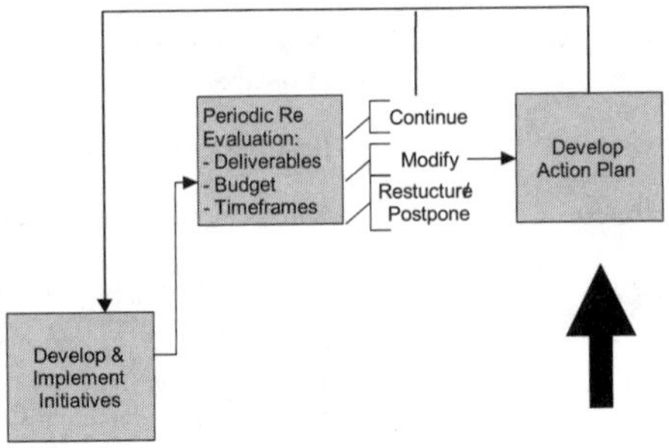

Figure 4.4.4   Develop Action Plan

CASE 2 Nicole Robertson – Clark Foods

Nicole Robertson is a newly-minted arrival at Clark Foods Corporation. Her previous employment was with a bio-tech company where Nicole had been a senior IT professional responsible for the IT strategic direction for the Customer Service Unit of the Waste Basin Manufacturing Company. Nicole operated the help desk and made sure that customer calls were handled in an efficient, professional manner. She had a group of top-notch, highly-educated professionals who would do anything to get the job done. She firmly believed she understood the concept of customer service. No matter what environment she worked in, she knew she would exhibit the same level of customer satisfaction that she believed was the cornerstone of any organization's survival and success.

A few months before arriving at Clark Foods, Nicole figured she could utilize her technical knowledge and know-how and not only be a stand-out, but to help the firm grow and prosper.

Nicole arrived at Clark Foods in December 1997 as its new senior IT Strategist for the *financial services unit*, which included functioning with the Tax, Treasury and the Controller's units. The *financial services unit* had a reputation of being harsh on IT. There was obvious bad blood between the two groups, basically caused by poor communication.

Nicole's day-one perception of the organization was that corporate and the business units all shared the same overall assessment of IT. She decided it would be a nice atmosphere to work and that there would be plenty of opportunity to make a difference.

At her thirty-day mark, Nicole realized that the service level given to process certain functions within her group had to increase from an IT perspective. Based on her 180-day assessment, things were in line and on target but some of the units under her function were not getting the level of help from IT that they needed. Her conclusion was based on the *business system plan process*, which she began four months after arriving at Clark.

Here are some of the activities Nicole completed to make sure she had a strategic document to use as a guide:

A) In her first month, Nicole performed an initial assessment of the overall organization by meeting with her clients.
B) The next month, January, she met with her key leaders from each process area: Treasury, Tax, and Controller.
C) In February Nicole gave a presentation to her process owners,

explaining her Business Systems Plan and what she was about to embark on.
D) In March, she met with each of her process owners to gather information.
E) In April the formal business systems plan process began and wrapped up in September.
F) Formal review of the plan's findings occurred in October with upper management.

Initial Assessment - Process Leaders Meeting

TREASURY

In late December, Nicole met with Chris Matthews, head of Treasury, and discussed her role and activities to be performed. Nicole thought that from a customer service perspective, she had to set expectations with her clients and customers to ensure that at the end of each deliverable, the expectations were met or, in her case, exceeded.

Her meeting with Chris went well, despite one big surprise. Nicole was unaware that her initial meeting with Chris would not only include Chris, but four other direct reports. She initially thought the meeting was an ambush, but that fear was quickly put to rest as she realized they seemed to be amicable business owners who were more interested in getting the work done than focusing on activities of the past.

Chris thought her role was positioned well relative to the other units. The Expense System was a major project currently being rolled out, and appeared to be going well. Chris mentioned that the APN upgrade of the treasury system was delayed, and was advised that the delay was a choice the group made until the expense system was completed. Other systems that Nicole discussed with the group were the cash management system, the asset risk software and other AS-400 applications.

Nicole was happy with what she heard from the group. They looked forward to working with her and gave her the support, direction and advice she needed.

TAX

During week number three, Nicole met one-on-one with Rich Fearer, the head of Clark's tax function and learned about the mixed feelings in his department toward IT. They felt they were not getting enough attention and also thought they were overlooked by Corporate.

Instead of belaboring the point, Nicole discussed with Rich things she could do to make IT more responsive to their needs. They discussed *record retention* and *fixed asset systems* as systems that could enhance the unit's functionality. They spoke about new technologies that would add value to tax by feeding the IRS directly via an electronic intermediary. Other systems mentioned were the *Big 4 tax system* and the *real estate tax system*.

Afterward Nicole created a list of activities that Rich and his department were expecting from her. She realized there were some "low-hanging" fruit that could be handled immediately by a maintenance support group that supported Treasury. Nicole left the meeting believing that she had a handle on the overall picture for Treasury. She did not want to focus on the minor activities, but thought it was important to focus her attention on the activities that were more strategic than tactical.

CONTROLLER

Nicole met with Myrold Hensen, Yuan Stenerough and Greg Bibenski who were in charge of the Controller's department. They discussed the various activities that the group was involved in. It was obvious that the group was responsible for too many tasks, but Nicole did not verbalize her thoughts. She could tell that at this point they couldn't see "the forest for the trees." Besides, the group seemed disinterested in what Nicole thought and were somewhat dictating a wish list to her. There was an atmosphere of non-partnership, and "one-upmanship".

Fortunately, Nicole was able to steer the discussion toward the topic of current and future systems. They focused on reporting needs for the controllers and the various users in the corporation. They needed some immediate reports from the AS-400 systems such as *Credit Union Reports, Reconciliation Reports and Deduction Credit Collection Reports*.

After completing her initial meetings, Nicole knew what each function needed. She had a sense of what needed to be handled tactically and the strategic matters that had to be dealt with. Her next step was to meet with IT consultant from Ernst and Young, Betty White, and have her deal with the tactical issues while she focused on the much-needed strategic matters.

Nicole knew of the *business systems planning process*. She met with Richard Krenna, head of the Project Office to discuss the process on the documents needed to complete the plan. From there, she went back to her office and created documentation that would help facilitate her meetings with each function as she developed the plans.

Presentation Created to Explain Planning Process

All IT strategists and directors at the firm had to perform the same function. Nicole thought it was a good idea to meet with each person to figure out what was the best way to go about explaining the process to her clients. She met with them in early January and then went back to her office to create a draft of the presentation for her clients. She thought if she could explain the process in a clear and concise manner, she would succeed. Her presentation documents included the following slides:

Business Systems Plan Process

Financial Services Unit
Clark Foods
February 2, 1998

What we will be discussing today...

- Why A BSP?
- BSP Overview and Process
- Discussion of Department Mission, Objectives and Goals
- Project Discussion
- Project List
- Inventory of Existing Applications
- Next Steps

Why A BSP #1?

- Align IT & Business agenda & strategies.
- Coordinate IT plans and related support across Clark Foods.
- Supply CIO/Business leaders with rational measures of investments being made.
- Performed for all other Business Units.

Why A BSP #2?

- Understanding and knowing the business in which people operate will be a key to success.
- Focusing on strategy and planning will in the long run lower costs, reduce redundancies and increase relationships and cooperation between the Business and IT entities.

BSP Overview

- Executive Summary
- Strategies and Objectives
- Initiative Planning
- Key Initiatives for the Coming Year
- Business Unit IT Landscape & Strategies
- Potential Key Initiatives

Business Unit Direction

- Mission
- Goals
- Objectives
- Strategies

Project Discussion
(for each)

- Support of Business Objectives
- Anticipated Timeframe(s)
- Resources (experts)
- Estimated $$ (if possible)

Project List
Draft - For Discussion Only!!

- Web Development and Deployment
- Expense Manager Launch
- Tax Management
- IRS TAX 2000
- Costing System Database Switch
- Treasury System Implementation

<table>
<tr><td>

Existing Application Inventory

- "Production" Applications
  - AS/400
  - RISC 6000
- Client/Server Applications
- Stand-Alone PC Applications

</td><td>

Next Steps

- Meet Business Unit Designees (today)
- Integrate forms to BSP Template (6/1)
- Validation from Business Unit (6/15)
- Identify Initiatives (7/15)
- Finalize BSP (8/1)
- Create & Finalize Budget

</td></tr>
</table>

The purpose of the slides was to help her clients walk though the process in a simple form. The documents included discussion points such as what is a BSP, defining objectives and goals, operational issues, and initiative development to drive the operational issues. Nicole felt that instead of going through a long drawn-out process, it was better to give her clients a sense of what the BSP was and then in subsequent meetings get from them, the specific information she needed to complete the planning document.

The meeting with each function occurred in early February and by all accounts, they went well. The feedback she received was that the functions got a sense she genuinely meant business. They mentioned that by going through the process, they felt a sense of partnership instead of being "dictated" to by IT.

Following each meeting, Nicole arranged separate future meetings to gather information for the BSP. She would meet with them individually, gather information about what they were looking for and proceed to develop the plan.

Nicole did not have to develop the Financial Services' goals, missions, objectives, market position, strengths, weaknesses, market opportunities, and potential competition in the market. Hamlet Enterprises a consulting firm, had been commissioned by the CFO to gather the business information for Clark Foods Corporation. Nicole was very grateful for this vital information, she knew that she could not proceed with the IT planning process unless the Financial Services business information was known and if she didn't understand the unit's direction.

Nicole was confident now that the individual functions knew where they were going, what they wanted, and understood the landscape. Now it was time to take all of that information, prioritize it, and determine the right path.

Meeting with Process Leaders

Nicole's meeting with the process owners, where she gathered specific information about projects needed for the upcoming year, went very well. The functional areas knew where they wanted to go and the projects they needed to do. The format for the meeting was general discussions around activities that should be done from an IT perspective to address the business issues and objectives. The processes for her meeting were:

1. Review with each member the findings of Hamlet Enterprises regarding objectives, goal-setting, and direction of the Financial Services Group.
2. Review each individual functional needs and how they fit in with the Group's overall direction.
3. Discuss possible process changes and actions that could be used to ensure they were moving in the right direction.
4. Discuss possible strategies to address the process changes that the units were seeking.

The format for the meetings was not to indulge in chalkboard writing and documentation; instead they focused on face-to-face discussion about the wants and needs of the business. Nicole always thought it was important to discuss technology as an after-thought, once she had understood the direction the business was headed.

Nicole's meetings with the Treasury and Tax functions went well. They understood and agreed with the findings from Hamlet Enterprises and quickly determined on their own the initiatives they were looking for—both short-term (within a year) and long-term (over a three-year period).

Nicole's meeting with the Controllers did not go as smoothly as she had wanted. One major sticking point was brought up repeatedly by Myrold Hensen—he was not clear whether the initiatives being discussed were local or global. He felt control from a corporate perspective was the Financial Services Group, but the projects that were developed had a global flavor. In the future, if the group proceeded this way, they believed that there might be a problem with the implementation of systems that were developed locally, but launched globally. In most of the discussion about possible initiatives for the upcoming year, the issue of scope was always on the agenda. For each initiative, it was dealt with by raising the local vs. global issue to the higher level in the organization. This issue had to be resolved quickly. Nicole deferred this to her boss, the vice president of IT. Likewise the Financial Services unit raised the issue to their management, the controller.

Planning Process Iteration

With all the information Nicole had gathered over the past month, she now had enough to put together a planning document. She knew the creation of the *Business Systems Plan* was not a one-shot deal. She developed a draft by documenting:

- *The Service Units'* goals, objectives, missions, strategies. She listed the various IT strategies that must be in place at Clark to ensure business success.
- She linked the business objectives with the IT strategies using the *Strategic Business Technology Alignment* table.
- She linked the IT strategies to the various IT initiatives by utilizing the *Strategic IT Alignment* table.
- Next, she linked the IT Initiatives back to the business objectives by using the *Strategic Business Alignment* table. This made it possible for no IT initiatives to be undertaken without first linking it to a business objective.
- Based on the discussions she had, she created a list of all the initiatives and placed them on a three-year agenda. This would be confirmed at the review meeting.
- She talked with her lower-level direct reports and vendors to find out cost, current technologies, and resources that it would take to complete the initiatives discussed earlier.
- She determined gaps in the process from where the organization was to where it was headed both from an IT and from a business perspective.
- She met with the chief technology officer to determine the future of the firm with respect to base technologies used on a daily basis to technologies in research at various organizations that Clark would be using.
- She met with Betty White, the head of Maintenance Systems, to help develop current architecture. She was the most experienced with the current platform that the Financial Systems unit had.
- She proceeded to develop a one-year picture and from there drafted the *Key Initiatives List* and *Categorization*.
- The final section of the *Business Systems Plan* dealt with the IT landscape and strategies. There she documented the support she had, common technologies being used, and possible shared technologies that she believed could be used across the organization.

By the end of August, she was ready for her presentation to the group. She reviewed all her documents and findings with her boss, Jeff Williplains. Following their review, they both met with the CIO, James Carter, to get his blessing. He mentioned it would be good to include the CFO, Jack Webb, at the final presentation.

The review meeting became the prioritization meeting. Nicole, Jeff, James and Jack Webb were there along with the head of each of the sub-units of the Financial Services Group: Chris Matthews, Treasury; and Rich Fearer, Tax; and Myrold Hensen, Yuan Stenerough and Greg Bibenski, Controller.

They reviewed the overall three-year picture and the items that were on the table for the following year. Jack Webb was the main decision and prioritization point. He reviewed all the initiatives and decided that the list was too long. He solicited feedback from the group before proceeding to move some of the initiatives on the one-year agenda to those of the next two to three years.

At the end of the meeting, they all agreed it was a very worthwhile process. Nicole now had an agenda of items and knew the business had agreed and signed off to IT on the *Business Systems Plan*. She had a list of tasks from a strategic standpoint that could help enhance the function of the Financial Services Unit.

All her hard work and dedication had paid off. She had been successful in her endeavor and now had a green light to proceed as planned.

Information Technology Plan (BSP) - Structure and Content

Like an architect designing a home, before one plans the kitchen or dining room one must decide on its layout and basic structure. What type of house he's building? How much square footage? One story or two? How many bedrooms? Will there be a two-car or a three-car garage? The future homeowner will want to know such things as the home's dimensions, its location, the size of the lot, etc.

Before the general contractor can even break ground to start construction on this home, there must first be an architectural drawing defining the layout, structure, and general design of the property. This helps everyone involved to see a high-level view of the home and the property.

An organization's *Business Systems Plan* is very similar. The components of the plan will give everyone involved a complete high-level view and a good understanding of all proposed. Let's take a look at the structural components of the *Business Systems Plan* and then look at its specific content.

5   *Plan Structure*

<u>The Plan Structure</u> on page 86, demonstrates a high-level structural view of a *Business Systems Plan* (BSP). Before we delve into the overall plan we will look at the structure. At its highest level, the BSP has four central structural components:

❑   Business Environment
❑   Overview and Systems
❑   Summary of Programs - The Initiatives List
❑   The IT Landscape.

5. 1   *Business Environment*

A

BSP: BUSINESS ENVIRONMENT OBJECTIVIES & STRATEGIES

The business environment focuses on the department, function and business unit for which the IT function is serving. For all purposes the business environment is the client of the IT function or department.

This part of the document demonstrates to the client:

1. Clear and concise understanding of how the business operates;
2. An understanding of the business's goals, missions, objectives and directon;
3. An understanding of the issues and challenges facing the business;
4. An understanding of the strengths, weaknesses, opportunities and threats that the business encounters on a daily basis;
5. An understanding of any internal or external regulatory activities affecting the business;
6. An understanding of any compliance-related issues that enables or deters the business from achieving its goals;

7. Linkages of the business objectives and strategies with that of the IT function.

Documenting these critical understandings is achieved through interviewing and significant face time with key business partners. The stewards of these documents are key senior executives who serve as key relationship managers with the business. The relationship manager must be involved in key strategic meetings of the business.

Relationship Managers are:

❏ Client-facing people who understand the business strategies of customers;

❏ Adept at working with IT resources to satisfy customers;

❏ Able to understand business requirements;

❏ Able to communicate the requirements to IT;

❏ Able to assure customer satisfaction with services.

In order to get a clear understanding of business objectives, goals and strategies, the senior executive or relationship manager must be involved in the day-to-day activities of their client. They should be forward facing and attend some, if not all, major strategic meeting with senior business leaders.

This 1) assures that the business involvement is necessary and 2) demonstrates a commitment to the business to understand the many-faceted activities they are involved in. It takes time for a relationship manager to get involved in the day-to-day activity of the business. This will be discussed more in detail on the relationship management section.

5. 2   *Overview and Systems*

```
B


BSP: SYSTEMS OVERVIEW
IT ARCHITECTURE,
1-3 YEAR PLAN
```

The overview gives a clear picture of the world of *information technology* and the documented plan of activities to be undertaken in support of the business. The overview includes the base technologies and their components that will be built for the business. It is not surprising in this part of the structure to discuss the one-year, the three- or five-year plan, and the overall architecture. This is to achieve the end-state of support needed for the business.

A key component of the end-state is that it will never be an end-state. Every three to five years, the overall outlook and architecture is reviewed and updated for another three to five years. Some might say that if there is no end-state, then IT will continue spending countless dollars on itself—thus creating a career for life.

The fact is, however, that any business will continue to invest in itself as the marketplace changes. *Information technology* is no different. The need for continued spending is not just a concept, but something that is a reality due to the changing nature of technology. Information technology re-invigorates itself every three to five years.

The architecture is the most important part of the system activities within the *Business Systems Plan*. The architecture documents the as-is and to-be state of the IT function and its support for the business.

There are three components to architecture as it relates to information technology: 1) data architecture, 2) application architecture and 3) technology architecture (Spewak, 12). These types of architecture are very similar to conventional architecture in that they involve blueprints, drawings, and models. They define and describe the data, applications, and technology needed to support the business (Spewak, 12). The architecture serves as the baseline activity to be undertaken by IT. The one-year view and the three- to five-year view gives a general understanding of the direction of IT initiatives that will be developed to assist the business.

For any business that *information technology* supports, these critical elements must be taken into consideration. Without investigating and documenting data, technology, people, or process needs of the business, the IT function would not be effectively addressing the important components necessary for business survival.

The Plan Structure

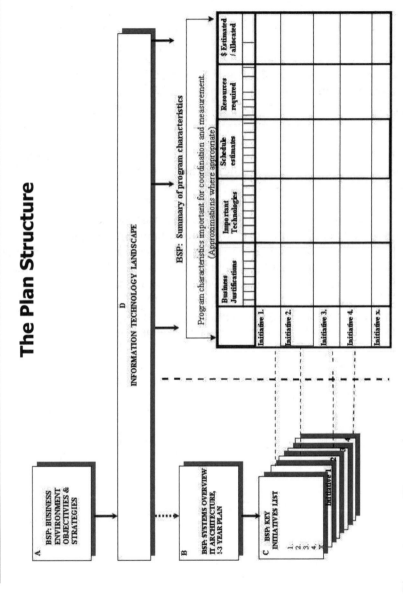

Figure 5. 1   The Plan Structure

5. 3   *Summary of Programs - The Initiatives List*

```
C    BSP: KEY
INITIATIVES LIST

1.
2.
3.
4.
X
```

Once you have a good understanding of the direction of the business and a clear direction as to where the IT is going in terms of an architecture and infrastructure, the next thing to focus on is the development of initiatives.

Initiative development is easy. Each and every stakeholder in *information technology*, if left to their own devices, could derive three to four initiatives on their own. Senior executives who read current wired magazines have been known to approach their IT colleagues demanding certain initiatives be developed. This can create an un-welcoming atmosphere for the IT function. The IT function should not ignore the new idea brought to them by the business, but it must be tempered considering the line-up of other activities the business is already performing.

The focus in the initiative development is to gather, develop and come forward with a list of IT initiatives that will serve and enable the business. The development of these initiatives could come from good sources such as competitors who have developed similar IT product and services or IT researchers who have already generated good solid technologies for the business.

The initiative list is not restricted and should not be based on the resources available. Too often companies look at the resources they have and limit their thinking based on the specific expenditures available. Instead, the individuals devising the list of initiatives should consider the following statement: "What would I do if I had unlimited funds and was able to do anything I wanted?" This leaves the thinkers with a freedom of thought to devise initiatives that will affect their world based on the direction of both technology and the business.

5. 4   *The Information Technology Landscape*

D
INFORMATION TECHNOLOGY LANDSCAPE

The IT landscape is the people, process, technologies and tools that are put in place by the IT function to support the business. The focus of the IT landscape is to effectively and efficiently ensure the business gets the enabling technologies that they need. The IT landscape will look at the structure of the organization. It will look at the leadership of the organization and how effectively it is aligned with the IT structure. It will look at the technology that will be used by IT. It will look at cutting-edge languages and technologies in the commercial world and determine how they can acquire not only the technology but the skill.   A comprehensive view should be done of the skills needed, given current technology and the futuristic view of technology in the industry.

In its simplistic form, the IT landscape is an organization assessment of the entire IT function. It discusses the futuristic environment within the function, taking a look at the culture and the definition of a successful culture and what it takes to be successful. Understanding the future needs with the IT function and key/critical success factors, IT can then look at the current culture. An analysis of the current culture will yield the gap between the current culture and the future culture that needs to be attained in order to be successful.

A further focus of the overall landscape is a look into common technologies the function possesses that can be cross-linked with enterprise-wide initiatives. Enterprise-wide initiatives are initiatives normally developed by "corporate" that will affect the entire corporation. A collection and analysis of these enterprise-wide initiatives provides opportunities for cost reduction by eliminating IT initiative redundancies. Additionally there needs to be a clear highlight of first-time use technology, which will help document any potential risk.

The Plan Content

The Business Systems Plan (BSP) content will detail its specific items, based on the structure developed on page 83. The content will review in definitional terms what the key sections of the BSP are. Following a definition or two, we will delve into their usage by presenting key examples.

6 Executive Summary

The *Executive Summary* is usually the final document in the overall plan.   The *Executive Summary* is written for the organization's executives, whether it is the CEO, CFO and/or COO. This enables them to gain an idea of the divisional IT initiatives.

The *Executive Summary* consists of five sections with each about two to three pages in length. The sections are: *1) Plan Overview, 2) IT Budget Expectation and Categorization, 3) Key Initiative List and Requirements, 4) Compliance and External Regulatory Initiatives, and 5) Other Important Items.* The *Executive Summary* can be examined by the following:

❑ **The Plan Overview**

Even though we will discuss this first, the *Plan Overview* is usually completed when the entire plan has been compiled and its author—the IT executive—is pulling together the document's content. The Plan Overview summarizes in one to three paragraphs the overall intent of IT in support of the business.

Examples

❑ *The Technology Services Unit for Safety, Health and Toxicology will produce an enhanced program that provides a High-Level of support to the internal customer and also extends to external customer. Within the last eight to nine months, majority of the focus has been on infrastructure issues and efforts to stabilize the environment for MSDS creation.   The major effort that began in 2003 around MSDS will be continued into 2004 and implemented in the year 2005. Within the next year a considerable amount of the budget will go toward spending on a new Toxicology and Product Regulatory Compliance system. Functionality assessment is completed, request for information executed and within the next few months, the focus will be on finalizing a vendor for this initiative.   The accomplishment of these initiatives will maintain the technology function's status as a source of business advantage to the company's Safety, Health and Toxicology Unit.*

❑ *The IT Services Unit for the Environmental Unit will produce an enhanced program that provides a High-Level of support to internal and external customers. Majority of the expense will be*

---

dedicated to supporting the manufacturing sites on a continuing basis. However, at least four major initiatives will be launched as follows 1) use of Intranet technologies for environmental information exchange, 2) improve tracking of toxic release inventory 3) identify and implement opportunities for pollution prevention and 4) improve environmental incident reporting with use of database technology. Additionally, there will be an increased focus on strategic items. Some infrastructure upgrade will be necessary; migration to enterprise standards will continue; and, database development effort will be a focus. Completing these initiatives will maintain the IT function's status as a source of business advantage to the Environmental Services Department.

❑ *The approach to the 2004 plan is one of stabilization and containment with a focus on "Electronic Office". Stabilization in terms of putting together enterprise solutions that focused on SQL Server access and an approach to centralization of databases. The "Electronic Office" will focus on a strategy of initiatives that takes into account the latest technologies that can enable the department to achieve its business objectives. After our initial assessment of the infrastructure needed for this plan, IT and Legal agree that focusing on any additional initiatives for this plan, IT and Legal agree that focusing on any additional initiatives for this year would be of value to Legal. As such the department will focus entirely on maintenance activity and final implementation of the contract writer system from 2004 in the year 2005.*

❑ *HealthCare Inc.'s discretionary IT resources in 2004 will be expended largely to support business initiatives focused on reducing medical costs and on developing tools and the infrastructure for a re-engineered operations environment to reduce operations cost and improve service levels. Electronic commerce, Internet, distributed systems, image and workflow technologies are some important technologies associated with key IT initiatives in 2004.*

❑ *2005 was a year of significant change for Company X Bank. The decision was made to exit the broad market credit card business to focus on Company X relationship customers and to redesign the organization structure around functions where historically the emphasis had been on products. At the present time the Bank is involved in a comprehensive strategic planning effort that will define the goals and tactics necessary to meet financial service aspirations. The challenge in this BSP process is too identify initiatives with long-term strategic value to the organization, while the businesses strategy itself is not yet complete.*

The Bank's BSP initiatives can be broken down into two broad categories: 1) initiatives that must be done in order to meet regulatory needs or to support on-going business activities and 2) initiatives that fit with the long-term strategic visions it is currently understood. Initiatives in the second category are electronic banking, telecommunication software upgrades, financial reporting system, upgrade network backbone, TS2 conversion, and auto dialer. As the strategy evolves we expect to make adjustments to the BAU environment that is appropriate from a staffing and capability perspective. The expenses attributed to the BAU environment are run rate projections from 1997 carried forward; they should be used for" scale" purposes only will be updated with plan numbers after a detailed budgeted is completed.

❑ **IT Budget Expectation and Categorization**

The IT Budget Expectation and Categorization is a simple chart that shows the amount of funds being spent on the initiatives and the category for each. When we build our own personal budgets, we divide our income into two categories: "absolute necessities (non-discretionary spending) and "optional spending" (discretionary spending). Companies are no different.

Funds to be spent on discretionary activities can be divided into two groups: strategic and infrastructure. Strategic spending improves an organization's business environment, enhances its market share, and affects other important business undertakings in a positive manner.

Infrastructure spending is spending on base-level systems that are needed in order to support application development and implementation. For example, an infrastructure endeavor could be the migration from one version of Microsoft application to another, the elimination of one operating system for another or the replacement of multiple e-mail systems for one standard system.

Within the different types of spending are sub-categories. The sub-categories under discretionary spending are: *a) Strategic Development (one-to-five years); b) Tactical Development (current year); and c) Infrastructure Development (baseline).*

The sub-categories under non-discretionary spending are: a) Salaries; *b) Depreciation and Maintenance; c) Other Business-As-Usual activities (those not accounted for in a-e); d) Year 20xx Activities (specific to year 2000 activity or any other industry-wide activities; and e) Corporate Allocations (charge-back by division from corporate technology unit). Definitions of these terms are in the appendix.*

The Capital Plan captures spending that is not expensed but can be capitalized and depreciated over time. Each business unit or corporate function summarizes their capital spending and those individualized line items are summed to capture an overall accumulated total for the entire enterprise. These capitalized initiatives can be amortized for the benefit of the business unit as well as the corporation.

The sum total of the divisional numbers and the corporate IT numbers will be different. In order for the division to show overall spending it must include all items under the discretionary category plus all the items under the non-discretionary numbers.

The difference between the division and corporate is that the Corporate IT allocation numbers will be shown and taken into consideration by the business unit, but will not be taken into consideration by corporate because that will be a double-count and expansion of the numbers.

Examples of the *IT Budget Expectation and Categorization* are found in Tables 6.1, 6.2, 6.3 and 6.4:

Table 6. 1   Corporate Safety Group – No Chargeback to Corporate

	20xx Budget ($000)		
	Discretionary	Non-Discretionary	**Total**
Strategic Development	1,700,000		**1,700,000**
Tactical Development	700,000		**700,000**
Infrastructure Development	400,000		**400,000**
Salaries		700,000	**700,000**
Depreciation, Maintenance		500,000	**500,000**
Business As Usual		300,000	**300,000**
Year 2000		200,000	**200,000**
Corporate IT Allocation		0	**0**
Total	**$2,800,000**	**$1,700,000**	**$4,500,000**

20xx Capital Plan	**$2,000,000**

In this example the corporate entity will be spending $4.5 million for the year, which consists of $2.8 million in discretionary and $1.7 million in non-discretionary spending. During 20xx, $200,000 was spent on Year 2000 system enhancement initiatives. The salary costs were $700,000. There was no corporate IT allocation because the safety function is a corporate group that supports all the businesses.

Table 6. 2   Utility Bank and Trust Business Unit

	20xx Budget ($000)		
	Discretionary	Non-Discretionary	**Total**
Strategic Development	1,576,000		**1,576,000**
Tactical Development	600,000		**600,000**
Infrastructure Development	800,000		**800,000**
Salaries		4,000,000	**4,000,000**
Depreciation, Maintenance		500,000	**500,000**
Business As Usual		300,000	**300,000**
Year 2000 Initiatives		700,000	**700,000**
Corporate IT Allocation		1,325,000	**1,325,000**
Total	**$2,976,000**	**$6,825,000**	**$9,801,000**

20xx Capital Plan	**$4,000,000**

The bank will be spending $9.8 million for the year 20xx. Due to its support activities it has a high non-discretionary spending of 70 percent relative to total spending. Since it is a banking unit of the overall corporation, it has IT allocations that are changes from the corporate IT function to the banking business unit.

Table 6. 3   Healthcare Business Unit

	20xx Budget ($000)		
	Discretionary	Non-Discretionary	**Total**
Strategic Development	14,000,000		**14,000,000**
Tactical Development	13,000,000		**13,000,000**
Infrastructure Development	7,000,000		**7,000,000**
Salaries		30,000,000	**30,000,000**
Depreciation, Maintenance		11,000,000	**11,000,000**
Business As Usual		20,000,000	**20,000,000**
Year 2000 Industry Initiative		6,000,000	**6,000,000**
Corporate IT Allocation		50,000,000	**50,000,000**
Total	**$34,000,000**	**$117,000,000**	**$151,000,000**

20xx Capital Plan	**$20,000,000**

The healthcare business unit during the year 20xx at Company X spent $151 million to manage its overall business unit IT function. As the organization gets bigger, there is a need for staffing whether internally or externally, hence the salary tends to be relatively high: $30 million or one-fifth of the overall spending. The larger the organization, the higher the allocation to corporate for its support of Healthcare's IT undertakings.

Table 6. 4   Corporate Information Technology

	20xx Budget ($000)		
	Discretionary	Non-Discretionary	Total
Strategic Development	5,000,000		**5,000,000**
Tactical Development	2,000,000		**2,000,000**
Infrastructure Development	4,000,000		**4,000,000**
Salaries		10,000,000	**10,000,000**
Depreciation, Maintenance		5,000,000	**5,000,000**
Business As Usual		4,000,000	**4,000,000**
Year 2000 Industry Initiative		0	**0**
Corporate IT Allocation		0	**0**
Total	**$11,000,000**	**$19,000,000**	**$30,000,000**

20xx Capital Plan	$8,000,000

The corporate IT unit does not have a charge-back to itself. In the above example, the overall cost of $30 million would be charged out to the businesses that corporate IT supports for its activities. In this example those activities are communication infrastructure, mainframe and server support for the businesses, setting standards and enforcing them, and developing architecture and planning activities for the overall corporation. The corporate unit in most cases tries to be slim and a well-oiled machine. Due to its continued support of the business, corporate tends to have a higher capital spending relative to its overall budget.

❑   **The Key Initiative List and Requirements**

At a High-Level the *Key Initiative List and Requirements* consists of a summary of all the initiatives to be undertaken by that particular business unit. The expectation is that this list should be small and consisting of about six to twelve initiatives. This list will be directly consistent with what the IT function defines as initiatives. In some organizations the key initiative list could be rather large because the unit insists on including small initiatives. Due to the possibilities of numerous and needless projects on the list, the organization must be clear, explicit, and concise in its definition of what constitutes a project. This helps with consistency between IT and the business unit. It also helps those who are responsible for rolling up all the information to give an enterprise view.

The Key Initiative List also documents requirements such as the resources required in terms of full-time employees, and the costs—both totals, what is already estimated and what is allocated to date. The difference between the estimated and the allocated will give those seeking funds a better understanding of the gap between what they have versus what they anticipate.

Criteria for Key Initiatives and Projects:
❑ Has a significant impact on meeting Business Unit's (BG) performance objectives.
❑ Requires resources to meet government-mandated requirements.
❑ Has a high visibility nature (internal or external) OR
❑ Fit one or more criteria of the risk profile:

  ❑ New technologies or development methodologies
  ❑ First use of a technology
  ❑ Cross business unit initiative
  ❑ Dependence on outside entities (vendors, consultants, third parties) for the success of the
    project
  ❑ Requires hardware or software R&D activities
  ❑ Does not conform with established standards of guidelines
  ❑ Needs infrastructure upgrades
  ❑ Major shift from old infrastructure to new infrastructure (e.g. shift from heavy printing to
    image and on-line report retrieval)
  ❑ Provides information access to external customers

Table 6. 5   Key Initiative List and Requirements

The Safety Group in the following chart will focus on system implementation and development around a new safety system. The cost allocated to the group is zero, hence the group will have to submit this list and total to its corporate entity for approval.

Initiatives	Required Resources		$ Estimated / Allocated ($000)			Return on Investment Justification
	Full Time Employees	Consultants	Total Project	20xx Estimated	20xx Allocated	
Reporting Incidents	2	2	0	0	0	Operational Necessity
Document Management	2	2	500,000	500,000	0	Operational Necessity
Scanning Initiatives	1	0	0	0	0	Operational Necessity
Safety and Environmental Strategy Assessment	1	2	0	0	0	Operational Necessity
Toxicology and Product Regulatory Compliance (TPRC)	1.5	2	0	0	0	Decrease legal risk exposure and cost for use of non compliant documents.
Software (SSDS System)	2	1	900,000	900,000	0	Decrease system maintenance cost.
System Implementation	2	2	1,500,000	1,500,000	0	Decrease legal risk exposure and cost for use of non compliant legal contract.
Data Conversion - SSDS	2	3	650,000	650,000	0	Increase efficiency and reduce cost for current manual research processes.
Training	1	0	400,000	400,000	0	Operational Necessity
Travel			250,000	250,000		Operational Necessity
Total	14.5	14	$4,200,000	$4,200,000	$0	

Table 6. 6   Financial Systems

Initiatives	Required Resources		$ Estimated / Allocated ($000)			Return on Investment Justification
	Full Time Employees	Consultants	Total Project	20xx Estimated	20xx Allocated	
General Ledger Implementation	26	2	4,062,000	4,062,000	0	Cost Reduction
SS subsidiary rollout	3	2	751,000	751,000	0	Cost Reduction and Operational Necessity
Financial Data Warehouse	11	4	2,352,000	2,352,000	0	Cost Reduction
Subledger/PGLS Frnt End	4	0	468,000	468,000	0	Cost Reduction and Operational Necessity
SS Budget--Development	2	0	234,000	234,000	0	Operational Necessity
Total	**46**	**8**	**$7,867,000**	**$7,867,000**	**$0**	

This unit is focusing on implementing financial and accounting systems to support various business units and the enterprise. The funds already allocated to this service unit are zero, which means that this is early in the planning process and the estimates will become the overall total cost.

Table 6. 7   Healthcare Business Unit

Initiatives	Required Resources		$ Estimated / Allocated ($000)			Return on Investment Justification
	Full Time Employees	Consultants	Total Project	20xx Estimated	20xx Allocated	
Affiliated Medical Groups	9	0	2,000,000	2,000,000	1,800,000	Strategic Necessity
Delegated Provider Program	29	27	7,000,000	7,000,000	6,000,000	Operational Necessity
Consolidation Program	13	8	2,100,000	2,100,000	1,000,000	Cost Reduction
Underwriting Desktop	11	10	4,000,000	4,000,000	3,000,000	Cost Reduction
Client/Member Internet Access	15	2	540,000	540,000	2,000,000	Market Share Increase
Year 2000	10	25	25,000,000	25,000,000	10,400,000	Strategic Necessity
FROGG Program	6	5	1,100,000	1,100,000	600,000	Strategic Necessity
EXCEL Migration Program	14	35	7,500,000	7,500,000	5,000,000	Operational Necessity
New General Ledger Program	6	5	3,100,000	3,100,000	2,600,000	Cost Reduction
Total	**113**	**117**	**$52,340,000**	**$52,340,000**	**$32,400,000**	

The Healthcare Business Unit will be rolling out numerous applications. Included in the *Application/Initiative List* is spending for client internet access during the 20xx spending cycle. There is a difference, however, between the estimated and allocated of about $20 million that the IT function will have to negotiate and prioritize with its business counterpart to arrive at a final concrete budget number.

❑ Compliance and External Regulatory Initiatives

Compliance and external regulatory initiatives are very important to capture. Due to the risk associated with these initiatives they often are "no-brainer" initiatives. These projects are funded without much analysis or discussion because the benefits and increased risks are so obvious.

Highlighting potential *IT-Enabling Applications* that can further the requirements of the business gives more validity to the IT initiatives and reduces the funding discussion. Caution must be taken because sometimes organizations categorize initiatives as regulatory and/or compliance when there is no evidence of either. For some IT professionals, it is deceptively used as a means to get a project approved without detailed analysis. Business counterparts need to be aware of this and ask the tough questions when the terms "compliance and regulatory initiatives" come up.

Examples

❑   *The following initiatives are being done to comply with external regulatory agencies: XRT Reporting, Pollution Prevention, and Environmental Incident Reporting.*
❑   *The Patent, Trademark and Agreement System and Forms Contract initiatives will help the department reach its goal of "electronic officing." This will place information at associates' fingertips and will assist them in meeting the departments' objectives.*
❑   *The CD Tax reporting initiative is the only bank technology initiative being driven by regulatory requirements. The initiative's objective is to modify the forms issued to customers from our third-party processor, M&I, and will be compliant with new tax regulations imposed on Corporate. Initiative's total cost is estimated at $62,000.*
❑   *TDX and XM State are initiatives based in compliance and external regulatory requirements. Without these initiatives we will have a higher risk of insurance defaults.*

❑ **Other Important Items**

There are times when the IT function needs to highlight important items that are not in the Executive Summary. Items included in this section, for example, could be a Year 20xx remediation effort and the cost associated with getting all systems changed to accommodate four-digit dates. The IT function might also address risk-related and organization-related matters that should be brought to the attention of the business.

Examples

❑ *There has been a lack of local support for the PC infrastructure within the unit, which has led to professional downtime and information redundancies. The technology follower position has improved within the last year. That issue will be addressed with improved coordination and dedicated personnel to the unit.*

❑ *The bank intends to move aggressively toward making its support infrastructure and processes compliant with corporate standards throughout 1998. Though not captured as discrete initiatives, taken together, the following projects will better position the Bank to fully integrate with corporate:*

   ❑ *The bank's IP Addressing will be converted to the corporate standard*
   ❑ *The bank's Intranet platform will be made corporate complaint*
   ❑ *The bank's database infrastructure will be made ready to support Sybase on a go-forward basis*
   ❑ *The bank will continue to change its desktop computing platform from the Macintosh to Windows as hardware is replaced or upgraded.*

❑ *The bank will convert Lotus Notes in the late 20x3/early 20x4 Above projects are being assumed as-business- usual activities and do not represent significant investment or staff time.*

Bringing the Section Together

A Comprehensive Example of the BSP Overview Section

Executive Summary

Business Systems Plan Overview

20xx was a year of significant change for Synergistic Bank. The decision was made for credit card business to focus on our core customers and to redesign the organization structure around functions. Historically the emphasis had been on products. The bank is now involved in a comprehensive strategic planning effort that will define the goals and tactics necessary to meet our financial and service aspirations. The challenge in this BSP process is to identify initiatives with long-term strategic value to the organization while the businesses strategy itself is not yet complete.

The bank's BSP initiatives then can be broken down into two broad categories: 1) initiatives that must be done to meet regulatory needs; or to support ongoing business activities and 2) initiatives that fit with the long-term strategic vision as it is currently understood.

Initiatives in the first category include *Imaging, Home Equity Loan Origination, and Deposit Tax Reporting.* Initiatives in the second category are *Electronic Banking, Telecommunication Software Upgrades, and Financial Reporting Systems.*

As the strategy evolves, we expect to make adjustments to the BAU environment that are appropriate from both a staffing and capability perspective. The expenses attributed to the BAU environment are run rate projections from previous year carried forward; they should be used for "scale" purposes only and will be updated with plan numbers after a detailed budget is completed.

Table 6. 8 Information Technology Budget Expectation and Categorization

	20xx Budget ($000)		
	Discretionary	Non-Discretionary	Total
Strategic Development	1,576,000		**1,576,000**
Tactical Development	600,000		**600,000**
Infrastructure Development	800,000		**800,000**
Salaries		4,000,000	**4,000,000**
Depreciation, Maintenance		500,000	**500,000**
Business As Usual		300,000	**300,000**
Year 2000 Initiatives		700,000	**700,000**
Corporate IT Allocation		1,325,000	**1,325,000**
Total	**$2,976,000**	**$6,825,000**	**$9,801,000**

20xx Capital Plan	$4,000,000

Table 6. 9 Key Initiatives List and Requirements

	Required Resources		$ Estimated / Allocated ($000)			Return on Investment Justification
Initiatives	Full Time Employees	Consultants	Total Project	20xx Estimated	20xx Allocated	
Imaging	10.0	7.0	1,500,000	1,000,000	0	Cost Reduction
Electronic Banking	5.0	1.0	400,000	500,000	0	Market Share Increase
Home Loan Initiative	0.3	0.5	794,000	700,000	0	Cost Reduction
Fin. Report Sys. Re-eng.	0.9	3.0	500,000	200,000	0	Cost Reduction
Upgrade Ntwk Backbone	3.0	3.0	708,000	700,000	0	Cost Reduction
Year 2000	2.0	8.0	200,000	200,000	0	Strategic Necessity
Foreign Exchange Conversion	5.0	1.0	250,000	200,000	0	Operational Necessity
Tax System	0.1	0.0	624,000	500,000	0	Cost Reduction
Total	**26.3**	**23.5**	**$4,976,000**	**$4,000,000**	**$0**	

Compliance and External Regulatory Initiatives

The Tax initiative is the only Bank technology initiative that is driven by regulatory requirements. The initiative's objective is to modify the forms issued to customers from our third-party processor to be compliant with new tax regulations imposed on the enterprise. The total cost of this initiative is $624,000.

Other Important Items

The bank intends to move aggressively toward making its support infrastructure and processes compliant with standards throughout 1998. Though not captured as discrete initiatives, taken together, the following projects will better position the bank to fully integrate with Finesty Corporation:

- The bank will modify its systems development methodology to comply with the emerging standard .
- The bank's Intranet platform will be made compliant.
- The bank's database infrastructure will be made ready to support Sybase on a go forward basis.

Questions for Synergistic Bank to Consider

1. Is the investment environment for IT clearly defined?

2. Is the difference between discretionary and non-discretionary spending clearly defined as it relates to the IT technology?

3. What is the total investment spending in technology?

4. With $2.9 million being spent on strategic, tactical, and infrastructure development, why is total project costing $4.9 million? What is the difference going toward?

5. How would you characterize and justify the investment in initiatives for the current year?

6. How would you characterize the spending on compliance and regulatory initiatives? Is it needed and why?

7. If Synergistic Bank was a business unit of Synergistic Holdings and you were its senior IT strategist, how would you follow through on a corporate edict to cut spending for the upcoming year? What would you target and why?

7 *Strategies and Objectives*

The Strategies and Objectives section is at the center of planning in terms of what it covers and the alignment and linkage activities to be undertaken between the business and its IT function. This section will document clearly and concisely:

1. Business Unit Mission
2. Business Unit Goals
3. Business Unit Strategies and Processes
4. Business Unit Objectives
5. IT Function's Strategies
6. Strategic Alignment Issues and Gaps

Many times "objective" is mistaken for "strategy." Other times, "goal" and "mission" are considered one in the same. As we delve into each category, let's examine the definitions of mission, goals, objectives, strategies, and processes.

❑ **Business Unit Mission**

A mission statement is an all-encompassing summary of the business. It delivers a decisive message as to what the organization represents and where it is going.

Examples

❑ *We protect and improve our customers' financial well-being by providing them with superior advice, products, and services.*

❑ *The mission of ELMAC is to provide (a) regulatory tracking and advice; (b) product safety information; (c) consulting in employee and process safety, toxicology, industrial hygiene, transportation safety crisis management, and emergency response; and (d) audit/oversight services to the company. All these services are provided to both external as well as internal customers.*

❑ *The Law Department's mission is to create competitive advantages for Synergy Corporation by providing high-quality legal services to our partners that enable them to accomplish their business objectives.*

❑ *As a part of Entreupy Group, Elias Bank's mission is to build loyalty with the bank's associates, business partners and targeted customers, and thereby increase the profitability of Entreupy and the bank.*

❑ **Business Unit Goal**

A goal is a singular statement or group of statements that clearly deliver to the stakeholder or outside party the summary focus of the enterprise. While the "mission" gives an all-encompassing statement of the enterprise, the "goal" builds on the all-encompassing view of the organization with some added direction.

Examples
❑ *The goal of this unit is to establish limited liability to the firm in areas of environmental and safety. The intent is to have the following:*   ▪ *No regulatory citations*   ▪ *No major process upsets*   ▪ *Zero Lost Time Accident Frequency; 1.0 IEA*   ▪ *No transportation safety or product shipping regulatory citations*   ▪ *All audit recommendations resolved in 12 months or less*   ▪ *Readily and widely accessible product safety information*   ❑ *The Legal Department's goal is to 100 percent support the enterprise along the following lines:*   ▪ *Sound legal advice*   ▪ Responsiveness to business unit needs.

❑ **Business Unit Strategy**

There is sometimes confusion over the differences between an objective and a strategy. The strategy is the pattern or plan that integrates an organization's major goals, policies, and action sequences into a cohesive whole (Quinn, 3). This results in the allocation of resources into a unique and viable position.

Examples
❑ *The strategy focus of Enterprise Financial takes on a holistic approach of its entire   product and functional mix of investment, mutual funds, annuities, asset management, and retirement services.*

Examples

□ **Investment Management**
- *Increase product offerings by using a "singular company" approach that draws on existing retail and institutional investment teams. Hire additional investment talent where needed.*
- *Improve investment performance by providing product breadth, depth, and consistency. Create investment process that routinely compares our portfolios to competitors'. Appropriate incentive plan that help us win in the marketplace.*

□ **Mutual Funds and Annuities**
- *Use streamlined product development process to introduce several annuity and mutual fund offerings during the next several years.*
- *Roll out a shared customer service platform to support mutual fund, annuity, and retirement service customers and sellers.*
- *Expand service hours, simplify and consolidate statement format, and increase frequency.*

□ **Institutional Asset Management**
- *Increase further share of clients' assets that the group manages. Expand beyond traditional institutional assets, usually held in the retirement plans (principally defined benefit) of large plan sponsors such as corporations and public employee funds.*
- *Increase offerings to the large institutional market.*
- *Strengthen offerings of competitive core products; index funds as well as global international investments.*

□ **Retirement Services**
- *Execute a distribution strategy that relies on access to the small and mid-size market through our investment banking arm and distribution partners and augmented by third-party brokers.*
- *Promote timely and responsive service. Client service will be further enhanced by establishing client-dedicated teams, improved transaction workflows, and extensive use of voice response, client remote access, and image management systems.*
- *Continue proactive participant communication and education.*

□ **The main focus strategies of the Construction Division of Allied Corporation:**
- *Build flexible and product-focused plants;*
- *Apply innovative technologies to achieve effective design;*

Examples

- *Leverage firms to help construction to execute capital plan;*
- *Implement globalized approach to project management;*
- *Maximize use of modular design, standardized technologies, and construction management technologies.*

❑ **Strategies to support the above objectives and end-result goals of the environmental functions:**
- *Advise and counsel on current and pending regulatory issues*
- *Audit performance to ensure compliance*
- *Manage remediation projects cost effectively*
- *Develop and evaluate environmental technologies*

❑ **The following are managed processes developed along functional lines to ensure that the Legal Department operates in a responsive and efficient manner**
- *Manage Legal Consultation - render consultation and advice with respect to all legal matters involved in the conduct of the business (except tax and collective bargaining).*
- *Select and Manage Outside Legal Department – manage outside counsel, conduct negotiation at pre-law suit stage; represent corporation without outside counsel in certain cases; determine strategies; and, advise as to trial/settlement decisions.*
- *Prepare Contracts – prepare, review, and approve contracts to be entered into by or on behalf of the Company or any of its subsidiaries.*
- *Manage Litigation and Claim*
- *Defend Third-Party Environmental Claims*
- *Supervise Corporate Records – Oversee and ensure smooth operation of corporate records for the Company.*
- *Procure legal advice from outside counsel in specific areas*
- *Research Legal Issues – oversee legal mattes as it relates to areas of antitrust.*
- *Advise the Corporation as to Minimization of Future Legal Exposure*
- *Administer/Manage Corporate Documents – construe and interpret all corporate documents such as certificates of incorporation, by-laws, indentures, loan agreements, resolutions and proceedings of board of directors and committees, compensation and benefit plans and corporate policies.*

❑ **Unified Healthcare of America business themes that have been**

Examples

developed to support the business unit's objectives are:
- *Medical Loss Ratio Reduction*
- *Operational Systems Reduction*
- *Increased Service Levels*
- *Sales and Marketing*
- *Planning, Control, and Compliance*

❑ **Business Unit Objectives**

In certain instances objectives and goals are used interchangeably. Goals basically expound on the objectives. It is good to have a singular goal with multiple sub-parts to that goal. Objectives are those multiple sub-parts. An objective states <u>what</u> is to be achieved and <u>when</u> results are to be accomplished, but they do not state how the results are achieved (Quinn, 3).

Most objectives can be either a singular statement explaining a specific activity or a detailed description. The content of each objective statement is more important than the length.

Examples

❑ *To accomplish the mission of the Unit, the following objectives are key to achieving success:*
- *Assure compliance with manufacturer safety/product regulations*
- *Improve employee safety performance*
- *Communicate product safety information more effectively with customer   information more efficiently*
- *Provide internal customers with readily accessible regulatory and pertinent technical information*
- *Improve timeliness of audit recommendation resolutions*
- *Limit losses and liability due to product distribution use and potential mis-use*
- *Assure cost-effective regulation by proactively working with trade associations and other associations*

❑ *The Objectives of the Fetienty Bank are:*
- *Achieve targeted financial returns by generating $10 billion in new asset growth, reaching benchmark credit quality and expense*

Examples

> *results, and a targeted financial return of 15% or better on equity with low volatility.*
> - *Enhance the brand by forming and sustaining high-quality partnerships with the business*
> - *units raising the perceived value of products and services available from Fetienty.*
> - *Focus on establishing the Bank as a recognized center for excellence, leveraging existing Bank infrastructure and maintaining a model control environment which preserves the integrity of*
> - *its brand name and image.*
> - *Build customer loyalty by offering products that have a high perceived value to targeted Fetienty's customers to increase the penetration of these customers. Increase the average number of products to per household strengthening customer loyalty and relationships. Achieving overall customer satisfaction ratings of 90% or better while increasing customer loyalty.*
> - *Build associate loyalty by becoming an employer of highly-skilled and motivated associates who understand and are excited about their role in achieving Fetienty's success. Measure overall employee and leadership ratings satisfaction of 75 percent or better.*

> ❏ *The immediate objective is to build a consumer-centric and profitable healthcare company. High-level initiatives supporting this objective are:*
> - *manage medical costs and quality;*
> - *Drive down operating costs;*
> - *Develop products and channels to grow and retain profitable members.*

> *More specific priority goals include:*
> - *Reduce medical loss ratio by 5 points;*
> - *Reduce administrative costs by 15-20 percent;*
> - *Improve administrative services profitability by $150 million via pricing;*
> - *Restore service levels to target.*

> ❏ *Key objectives of the financial management group of S. Corporation include:*
> - *General Ledger Implementation*
>   - o *Implement the General Ledger effective January 1988;*

Examples
o   *Complete critical path extended tasks;* ■ *1996 exhibit reconciliation and 1997 Validation* o   *1997 life validation;* o   *Implement consolidation and fixed asset modules;* ■ *Coordinate with accounts payable implementation* o   *Implement CAPP procedures for AP accounts;* o   *Implement SmartStream expense reporting with AP;* ■ *Further development and implementation of financial controls;* ■ *Enhance reporting tools for complex exhibits and schedules through Data Warehouse;* ■ *Implement budget allocation vs. budget reporting;* ■ *Redesign structure of records and investment and expense allocations;* ■ *Develop key enterprise accounting policies, procedures and standards.*

❑ **Processes**

   Within each department or function there are processes that must be followed and adhered to, to ensure the success of that entity. Processes define the main functions of an entity and what it does on a day-to-day basis. Processes from an IT perspective could be System Life Cycle methodologies that are followed, for example, package implementation, custom development, re-engineering, or infrastructure activities. On the business side (finance, safety, legal, supply chain, investment), there are also business processes.

Examples
❑ *In order for the Safety function to be successful, the following processes must be in place and aligned with the overall strategy and objective of the function. They include the management of:* ■ *Product Stewardship* ■ *Regulatory Requirement* ■ *Personnel Health & Safety* ■ *Process Safety* ■ *Health & Safety Transportation Issues* ❑ *Processes of the Commercial Paper Divisions include:*

Examples
<ul><li>*Develop and Commercialize Technology*</li><li>*Create Diversified Markets*</li><li>*Manage Customer Relationships*</li><li>*Plan Production Operations*</li><li>*Manage Supply Sourcing*</li><li>*Process Orders*</li><li>*Produce Products*</li><li>*Manage Inventory and Distribution*</li></ul>

When alignment issues are discussed later in the book we will see that the IT strategy can be aligned to either the business strategy or the process. In most cases, it is better for the IT strategy to be aligned with the business strategy than for the IT strategy to be aligned with the process. From a planning perspective, it could be aligned with either. That said, the decision to do so rests with the IT executive level.

❑ **Information Technology Strategies**

IT strategies as its name implies, are strategies developed by the technology entity in support of the business. It is important to understand the business first and foremost before discussing any activity related to technology. In most cases, the CIO and senior level IT executives agree there is no need to focus on technology strategy without a thorough understanding of the business.

This requires a focus and a detailed understanding of the business in terms of its strategies, objectives, goals, etc., and an analysis of the business before investigating and documenting strategies that will enable the business. After a thorough understanding of the business, the IT function can focus on strategies that will enable the business. Examples of these strategies are as follows:

Examples

❑ *IT Strategies of Alliance Equity to ensure market leadership:*
    ■ *Integrate customer access*
        ○ *Create an infrastructure for customers to receive information, solve problems or manage their accounts; across all Alliance Equity's products and services.*
    ■ *Intelligent Work Stations*

Examples

> o *Provide desktop access to all customer data, including work or transactions in process, at the individual customer level. This tool will enable the other four strategies.*
>
> ▪ *Workflow Across Departments*
>> o *Establish integrated workflows across departments, processes, product, and service streams that enable customers to get information, solve problems, or manage their accounts with one contact.*
>
> ▪ *Expanded Imaging Technology*
>> o *Achieve paper-independent customer transactions across all business processes.*
>
> ▪ *Field Technology Platform*
>> o *A single platform for field offices that enables reliable and consistent customer transaction processing for any Alliance offering; field and sales support (leads, promotions, product information, etc.); home office communications and management reporting.*

❑ **To accomplish the Legal Department's business goals and objectives, the IT Function will develop the following key strategies to reach its target:**
  - ▪ *Provide mechanism for information exchange with internal/external customers and for information storage and retrieval.*
    - o *Replacement systems viability*
    - o *Data modeling and architecture*
    - o *System functionality*
  - ▪ *Identify and implement alternatives for new systems technology to improve legal processes:*
    - o *Data Storage/Retrieval*
    - o *Document Management*
    - o *Electronic Data Interchange*
    - o *Electronic Commerce*
    - o *Optimize system integration through evaluation of systems architecture and provide solutions for current/ongoing system:*
    - o *Minimize number of interfaces*
    - o *Global access*
    - o *Limit information redundancy*
    - o *Provide agenda for IT- related training for application and new systems upgrade.*

Examples

❑ ***Set strategic direction of the Fizz Corporation's IT Division:***
  - *Develop a unified technical architecture and technology standards*
  - *Conduct research into emerging technologies to gain earliest business advantage and give the best new-technology advice to the business groups*
  - *Develop a unified Lotus Notes and Internet/Intranet architecture, standards, and company direction for their use*
  - *Define and implement an integrated planning process that includes necessary data and process models and a living BSP process*
  - *Implement business measurement processes for IT function that gauge progress toward World Class*
  - *Implement IT community-building strategies and internal and external communications strategies to promote teamwork, and sharing of ideas, resources, and people across the IT community*
  - *Develop and implement company-wide process, methodology, and project management standards.*

❑ **Strategic Alignment Issues and Gaps**

This section analyzes the impact of completing the business goals, strategies, objectives, mission, and IT strategies. It addresses any areas that have to do with the overall strategies and objectives of the business unit. The focus here is on any activity that correlates with objective to strategy, goals to mission, or IT to business.

At this point the strategist states clearly any issue that could have a negative or enhanced impact on the overall direction of IT.

Examples

❑ ***Strategic Issues for Royal Financial Resources:***
The shift in strategic direction for the bank created many issues and concerns that are addressed directly within the context of our planning activities. Below is a summary of the strategic issues faced by the bank's IT functions:
  - *Linking IT strategy to business strategy: Since the bank's business strategy is not yet fully evolved, the IT organization will have to maintain a High-Level of flexibility in order to respond to business*

Examples

needs in 20xx. Additionally, the BSP will need to be maintained on an ongoing basis to reflect the changing business situation.

- *Staff Retention: The sale of the consolidated market portfolio teamed with a general organization redesign aimed at shifting the bank from a product-centric structure to a functional structure will result in staff reductions. The ability to retain high potential and critically skilled staff is vital to the future of the Bank's IT organization. A retention plan is in place at the bank through February 20xx and the compensation plan will be rolled out before the end of 1999. These two factors should help mitigate unwanted staff turnover in the short term.*
- *Mixed Desktop Platforms: The bank's current desktop computing platform is a*
- *Macintosh. The last Mac was purchased in March 20xx; tactical deployment of Windows NT machines has begun. The economics make a mass migration to NT in 1997 unfeasible. A challenge to the bank's IT organization will be to maintain a dual platform environment until 20xx when the last Mac's are fully depreciated.*

❑ *Prior to 20xx, there was limited spending on IT-related activities. Spending required to "keep the lights on" for business-as-usual activities has been limited and will remain so for the foreseeable year. The move now is to focus on strategic items thatwill help the environmental unit reach its ultimate goal of providing, storing, and archiving environmental information for Mentyce associates. The IT support necessary for all these initiatives is the most important strategic issue that needs to be addressed on a continued basis. The short-term focus is to use consultants from a strategic standpoint to address tactical issues. The focus will be on ensuring that staff has tools and knowledge to ensure the protection of company knowledge and intellectual properties. In 20xx there was a major focus on infrastructure development that was only a partial success due to lack of support. In 20xx we would like to improve the support beyond the 20xx levels.*

❑ *Strategic issues facing the Healthcare entity IT organization include building the IT staff as part of the final phases of the IT Transformation effort; designing and implementing the systems infrastructure to support changes to the business units' financial and legal structure; building and supporting applications for a re-engineered world-class operational environment; and, proactively and aggressively supporting changes within the healthcare industry.*

Examples
❑   *Various strategic issues that must be addressed by Yarn Inc. include: 1) retaining staff and acquiring new technology skills; 2) existing IT infrastructure is outdated and not in a position to support internal business management needs of "World Class" upgrades; 3) expanding distribution channels; and 4) expanding the ways customers can do business with us.*

Bringing the Section Together

A business unit or enterprise first needs to define its mission. Next, there are various goals that must be met to reach its mission. There will be strategies and objectives that are assigned and linked to the goals. Finally, there are processes put into place that must be followed by projects, and activities to ensure adequate alignment from top to bottom.

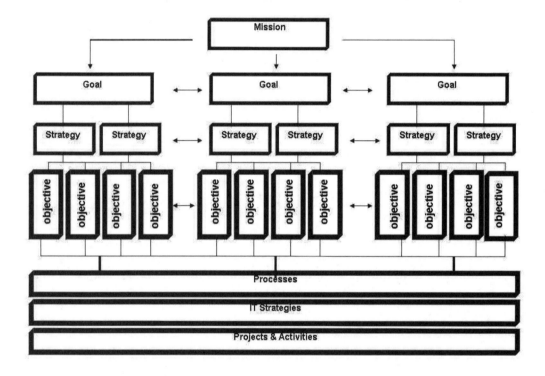

Figure 7. 1   The Mission-To-Project Flow

A comprehensive example of the *Strategies and Objective Section of Business Systems Planning* is as follows:

Strategies and Objectives

Business Unit's Mission
Clarion Enterprises' business philosophy embraces a global dedication to the health and safety of our employees, our

customers and our neighbors, and to the protection of environment.

We will strive to:

- Conduct our business in a manner that consistently demonstrates and renews this commitment;
- Obtain from our suppliers this same commitment;
- Design, build, operate and maintain our facilities to be safe for our employees, neighbors, and the environment;
- Manufacture our products in compliance with all appropriate regulations and, in many cases, exceed these requirements;
- Pursue technologies that foster materials' recovery and energy conservation while minimizing waste generation and environmental releases;
- Ship our products in safe and environmentally sound packaging.

Business Unit's Goals

The goal of this unit is to establish limited liability to the firm in areas of environmental, safety and health. The intent is to have the following:

- No EPA regulatory citations;
- No major environmental releases;
- All audit recommendations resolved or a plan in place in six months or less;
- Readily and widely accessible product environment and regulatory compliance information;
- Manage remediation liabilities cost-effectively.

Business Unit's Objectives

The following objectives are key in achieving success in accomplishing the unit's mission:

- Improve employee environmental awareness and performance;
- Provide customers with product environment information more efficiently;
- Provide internal customers with readily accessible regulatory compliance information;
- Improve timeliness of audit recommendation resolution;

- Limit environmental losses and liability;
- Manage remediation within scope of business plan.

Business Unit's Strategies/Processes

Strategies to support the above objectives and end-result goals are as follows:

- Advise and counsel on current and pending regulatory issues;
- Audit performance to ensure compliance;
- Manage remediation projects cost-effectively;
- Develop and evaluate environmental technologies;

Key Information Technology Strategies

IT strategies required to enable the business function:

- Provide mechanisms for information distribution to internal/external customers
  o Environmental information
  o MSDS information
  o Regulatory information
  o Training notices;
- Evaluate systems architecture and provide solutions for data storage and retrieval to current systems
  o Personal databases
  o Remediation database
  o Audit database;
- Implement system activities to support communication and information exchange;
- Evaluate and provide alternatives for efficient business information storage via document management and scanning facilities.

Strategic Alignment Issues/Gaps

Before 20xx there were limited dollars spent on IT-related activities. The dollars required to "keep the lights on" for business-as-usual activities have been limited and will remain so throughout the year. The move now is to focus on strategic items that will help the environmental unit reach its ultimate goal of providing, storing, and archiving environmental information accessible to Clarion associates.

Questions for Clarion Enterprises to Consider:

1. Does the mission statement belong to Clarion or its *Safety and Environmental* function?

2. What is the difference between Clarion's *Safety and Environmental* function's mission and goals?

3. How important is the *System Architecture* in the deployment of further IT applications?

4. How important is investing in IT at the corporate level with that of the strategic direction of the *Safety and Environmental* function?

5. Define possible actions that can be taken given the gaps that exist?

6. As an influential IT strategist, how would you approach the issue of strategic investment in technology if your area of operations is in the service unit?

7. How would you characterize the overall IT strategic direction of the *Safety and Environmental* function?

8   *Planning the Initiatives*

Before initiatives are executed there must be a gallant effort to ensure that IT's strategies and objectives are aligned correctly. This is what we call *alignment and execution* activities. Before we document the alignment activities, we should note that this section will capture the following items:

1. Strategic Business Technology Alignment
2. Strategic Information Technology Alignment
3. Strategic Business Alignment
4. Pictorial View: Three-Year Plan
5. System Architecture Diagram

There are three alignment activities that must be completed: 1) *Strategic Business Technology Alignment*, 2) *Strategic IT Alignment*, and 3) *Strategic Business Alignment.* The strategic planner has the option to perform all three alignments at once, or choose to perform them separately as each relates to the overall strategy.

Before performing the alignment activities, the initiatives lists (list of IT initiatives for the year) must be completed. It is recommended, as part of the process, that the initiatives list be gathered before going on to performing the alignments. This will be discussed in the Process Section of the book.

Figure 8. 1   The Alignment Link

The **Alignment Link**, if correctly implemented and utilized, enables the IT professional to focus not just on technology for technology's sake, but also on the usage of technology to enhance and further the business. With this focus on the business, IT not only performs its initiatives, but it looks to the business to be a driver of its objective.

Figure 8. 2   The Strategic Business Technology Alignment

❑ **The Strategic Business Technology Alignment (A to B):** From a process perspective this is the analysis of the appropriateness of the *IT Strategy to the Business Objective*. The strategic planner helps the business to address business issues and drives the business through workshops to arrive at the alignment. In step fashion, a chart is created documenting all the appropriate business objectives.

On the vertical side of the chart are listed all the key IT strategies. The strategic planner then walks the business through a list of tough questions to help them determine just how important each business objective is to the IT strategy. These are ranked on a scale of 1 to 5 or 1 to 3.

The summary of these numbers on the vertical and the horizontal table *(see below)* will give each stakeholder a good understanding of the linkages and the relevancy of IT strategies to the objectives. For example, one question a certain company might ask is, "How important is deploying sound databases for immediate access across a wide area network *(IT Strategy)* on the drive to expand sales into a developing country in Africa *(Business Objective)*?" Each would be given a number. The total may lead to discussion. Let's look at a few examples of *Strategic Business Technology Alignment*:

Table 8. 1 Financial Entity

IT Strategies	General Ledger Deployement across US	Coordinate Effective Payable Systems	Budget Improvements	Manage Financial Cost	Drive Down Operating Cost	Develop and Deploy Communication Channels	Deploy Policies	Objective 8	Objective 9	TOTAL
Provide mechanism for Integrated Access across IT platform	1	1	1	3	0	2	2			10
Provide desktop access to all customer data - transaction and IP	1	0	3	3	0	1	0			8
Evaluate and provide alternatives for efficient business information storage via document management and scanning facilites	2	2	0	2	2	0	0			8
Deploy where possible, integrated e-business solutions	0	0	0	3	3	3	3			12
Develop and Deploy a comprehensive field operation technology platform	1	1	1	2	2	2	0			9
Implement a cross business training platform for all employees	2	2	2	2	2	2	2			14
	7	6	7	15	9	10	7			

Table 8. 2 Legal Concerns

IT Strategies	Business Objectives									
	Perform Legal Services	Work with Business Units	Ensure Skills and Resources	Preventative Law Agenda	Manage Corporate Records	Objective 6	Objective 7	Objective 8	Objective 9	Objective 10
1. Provide mechanism for information exchange with internal/external customers	3	1		2	3					9
2. Ensure Legal Departments system long & short term going concern issues are addressed	2	1	2		3					8
3. Identify and implement alternatives for new systems technology to improve legal processes	3	2	2	1	2					10
4. Optimize systems integration through evaluation of systems architecture and provide solutions for current/on-going system	3	1		1	2					7
5. Provide agenda for IT related training for application and new systems upgrade	3		3	1	3					10
TOTAL	14	5	7	5	13					

Table 8. 3 Safety Concerns

IT Strategies	Business Objectives									TOTAL
	Assure compliance with Safety Regulatoin	Communicate Safety Information	Improve Safety Performance	Provide Readily Access Information at Fingertip	Improve Timeliness of Audits	Limit Losses and Liability	Proactive Working with Associations	Objective 8	Objective 9	
Provide mechanism for information to internal & external customers	3	1	3	3	0	2	2			14
Ensure system long & short term going concern issues are addressed	3	0	3	3	0	1	0			10
Evaluate and provide alternatives for efficient business information storage via document management and scanning facilites	2	2	0	2	2	0	0			8
Evaluate systems architecture and provide solutions for current/on-going Business systems	2	2	1	0	2	2	0			9
Provide agenda for IT related training for application and new systems upgrade	2	2	2	2	2	2	2			14
TOTAL	12	7	9	10	6	7	4			

The financial entity example focuses on six IT strategies for future implementation. The objectives range from *General Ledger Deployment to Deploying Policies* that will help with the dissemination of information. From an alignment and impact perspective, the two strategies listed above as "deploy where possible, integrated e-business solutions" and "implement a cross-business training platform for all employees" are in tight competition for resources reserved for IT initiatives. The Internet plays a major role with this concern as it plans to roll out application and initiatives that will be across platform and across a wide audience. If all the resources were properly allocated across the business objectives, the "Manage Financial Cost" is a focus of the entity for the upcoming period.

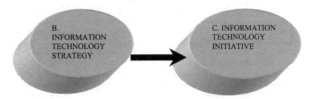

Figure 8. 3   The Strategic IT Alignment

❏ **The Strategic IT Alignment (B to C):** This alignment is no different than the one above. However, in this case it is the intent of the strategist to align IT strategies with the initiatives. A key point is that in the development of the overall BSP, this alignment activity cannot be done until all the initiatives are laid out for the entire three- or five-year period and then prioritized on a one-year schedule. This is extremely important from a process perspective; it must be completed after the initiatives have been formulated. Aligning IT strategies with phantom initiatives makes no practical or academic sense. If a strategic planner attempts this alignment activity without clearly defining the initiative development explained in the process steps on page 123, they are headed for failure.

❏ The B-C step is executed in a similar fashion to the A-B Alignment. The strategist begins with a blank chart with IT strategies listed horizontally and IT initiatives listed vertically. Generally speaking, there can be five to seven strategic items. Anything more will lead to questions whether or not the strategy items are clearly defined. If this occurs, there needs to be further scrutiny of the strategy development and the prioritization that led to finalization of those strategies.

❑ An initiative can support one or more strategies. Likewise, multiple strategies can be executed via one or more initiatives. Here are some examples of the *Strategic IT Alignment*:

Table 8. 4   Financial Entity

Initiatives	Information Technology Strategies									TOTAL
	Provide mechanism for Integrated Access across IT platform	Provide desktop access to all customer data - transaction and IP	Evaluate and provide alternatives for efficient business information storage via document management and scanning facilities	Deploy where possible, integrated e-business solutions	Develop and Deploy a comprehensive field operation technology platform	Implement a cross business training platform for all employees				
Ledger Development	3	1	1	1	0	2				8
SS subsidiary rollout	1	0	1	2	0	1				5
Data Warehouse	3	0	3	3	3	2				14
Sub General Accounting	1	0	1	1	0	2				5
Payable Depoyment	1	0	1	1	0	1				4
TOTAL	9	1	7	8	3	8				

Table 8. 5   Safety Entity

Initiatives	Provide Mechanism for Information Exchange	Replacement Systems Viability	Identify and Implement new system technology to improve process	Global system long term going concern are addressed	Evaluate and Provide alternative for Information Storage via document management	Evaluate System Architecture and provide technology savvy solution	IT Strategy 7	IT Strategy 8	IT Strategy 9	IT Strategy 10
Incident Reporting	3	0	0	3	0	1				7
Document Management	3	2	3	2	1	1				12
SCANTD Initiatives	1	0	0	1	0	1				3
Safety System Deployment	3	3	0	3	0	1				10
Labeling System (FDA)	3	3	0	1	1	1				9
EMERGENCY Response	3	3	0	0	0	1				7
AXT System Conversion	3	3	0	0	0	1				7
TOTAL	19	14	3	10	2	7				

The column group above is headed **Information Technology Strategies**.

In the above example of a financial entity, the most important initiative flowing out of the evaluation of the alignment activities is the *Data Warehouse* initiative. The most important strategy being addressed is to "provide mechanisms for *Integrated Access* across IT the platform." This is not the ultimate solution in determining which system and initiative to work on. However, it does send a clear signal to the IT strategist and to the business stakeholders that each counterpart has a clear understanding as to what is important. This B-C step is one leg of the A-C, B-C, and C-A triangle. They must all be done before an overall evaluation can be made as to the important priorities for that entity.

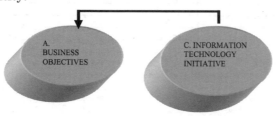

Figure 8. 4 The Strategic Business Alignment

❑ **The Strategic Business Alignment (C-A):** Once the business objectives have been defined and once the IT initiatives have been identified, the next step is to ensure that there is adequate alignment between the defined objectives and the initiatives. This is achieved through discussions between the business stakeholder and the IT strategist. From a process perspective, this is the most difficult part of the alignment issue. During the analysis the focus is on the responses to the potential alignment questions of initiatives to objectives and the elimination of thought processes related to *the need* to have a project versus *the want* to have a project. By this, we mean that at times certain stakeholders want projects for whatever reasons they deem fit. During discussion it can be determined that the need that once existed is not a need anymore, but something based on some unfounded and relatively low return and low value rationalization. The process activity related to the alignment of the objectives to strategy is defined more clearly in Section 8. Here are some examples of the *Strategic Business Alignment:*

Table 8. 6 Insurance Entity

| Initiatives | Business Objectives | | | | | | | | | TOTAL |
	Develop Brand	Customer Relationship	Enhance Distribution	Operational Improvements	Defined Products	Externally Focused				
Intranet Deployment	1	1	1	3	1	2				9
Chargback Initiative	1	2	1	2	1	1				8
Chargeback Finance	1	1	1	3	3	2				11
Customer Relationship System	2	3	3	1	1	1				11
Amalgamated Product System	1	2	2	1	3	2				11
PDA Rollout	3	2	3	2	1	1				12
Service Improvements	2	2	3	3	2	1				13
Brand Development System	3	3	2	2	3	1				**14**
Total	14	16	16	**17**	15	11				

Table 8. 7 Healthcare Concerns

	Business Objectives									
Initiatives	Financial Targeting	Brand Development	Build Customer Loyalty	Build Associate Satisfaction						TOTAL
Documenum & Imaging	2									2
Electronic Banking		2	2							4
Home Equity Systems	3	2								**5**
System Re-Engineering	2	1								3
Infrastructure Deployment		1								1
Intranet Upgrade		2								2
Vision 2000		3								3
ADB Conversion		2	2							4
Tax System		3								3
Autodialer		1								1
Total	7	**17**	4	0						

Table 8. 8 Finance Entity

	Business Objectives								
Initiatives	General Ledger Implementation	Management Reporting and Analysis	Financial Standards	New Method of Payments	Closeout Transaction	Debit Transaction Enhancement			TOTAL
Ledger Development	3	3			3				9
SS subsidiary rollout	1	1			3				5
Data Warehouse	1	3	3	3		2			**12**
Sub General Accounting		1	1	1		3			6
Payable Deployment		1							1
Total	5	9	4	4	6	5			

In close examination of the Healthcare Concerns we see that the "*Home Equity Systems*" has the greatest impact on the combined strategies of the concern. We see that summarily though, the most important strategic activity for healthcare is *"Brand Development."* A decision will have to be made regarding the impact of the importance of initiatives to strategies. At the end of the day, it is the resource money available to complete the initiatives that is going to drive the focus of the IT department for the upcoming years.

❑ **Pictorial View - Three-Year Plan**

The three-year plan, as its name implies, is a summary of all the activities to be accomplished over a three-year time span. The time span is relegated to three years primarily because of the rapid changes in technology.

Some organizations cast their vision on technology for a three- to five-year time span. Very well—it all depends on the industry that the organization is involved in. In some cases, an organization might venture to have more than a five year time span.

Estimations are that usage of technology and the need for technology in the financial services industry exceed that of the chemical industry. The primary driver is data and the need for the processing of that data at a quicker speed. In the pharmaceutical industry, where regulations and rules apply more distinctly than in the chemical industry, the need is for more cutting-edge, document-related technology. Again, the key is to let the industry dictate the level and the planning horizon for technology implementation and usage, thus the length of the pictorial view.

If we examine the exact planning horizon, the expectation is that the utilization of technology over a time horizon will show some kind of a trend. The importance of having the three-year plan in the documentation is that it clearly states the direction in which the entity is headed. In certain cases, the technology strategist will demonstrate to the stakeholders the utilization of their resources through the pictorial depiction of the expectation of initiative development and deployment. Here are some examples of typical three- and four-year plans:

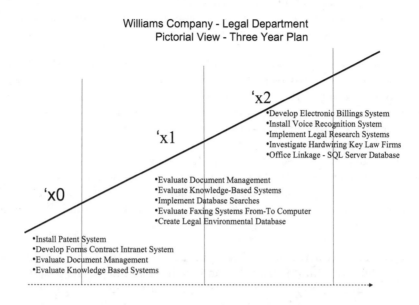

Figure 8. 5 Legal Entity

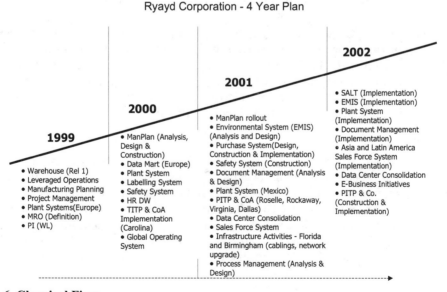

Figure 8. 6 Chemical Firm

An examination of a plan shows that in the left corner we begin with a certain year and an increasing scale over time. The activities and initiatives increase or decrease, depending on the strategy of the IT department.

In the example above, Ryayd Corporation is a manufacturing company with global operations from Asia Pacific to Europe to the United States. Unlike the Ryayd example, the other example of the Williams' Legal Department focuses on a three-year plan for one function within that corporation. Ryayd is focusing on the rollout of plant systems, manufacturing systems, environmental systems, and sales force activities. With Ryayd, there is a focus on methodology phases within projects. Using stages within methodology demonstrates to stakeholders that there is a bona fide process in place, ensuring that proper steps are being taken for successful completion of projects. It also sets the stage of understanding and communication as it relates to project status.

❑ **System Architecture Diagram.** IT architecture, in its simplistic form, is the blueprint and foundation on which all technology is designed, built, and maintained. As mentioned earlier, it's quite similar to the actual building of a house. An architect puts plans together and brings to fruition the idea that the owner has in mind. The architect designs the home by focusing on such base elements as columns, foundation, structures, bricks, tiles, etc. In a similar way, IT architecture, the "architect" reviews standards and looks at how things should be designed and ultimately built.

❑ IT architecture tells the story—from an IT perspective—of the overall big picture of what is being attempted and how the initiatives fit within the design of the big picture. Architecture, in most companies, is focused around three main areas: data, process, and technology. A story needs to be told and a map drawn regarding the direction and the intended implementation of the various IT initiatives.

Engineering Entity
❑ We will use the examples below to focus on architecture and its component. They focus on a company called Shadow Corporation, which has an engineering group that is responsible for designing buildings that will be built to manufacture the company's product. Shadow engages outside entities to complete the design work that was created internally. At the highest level, the key strategies in the company focused on presenting the architecture in three simplistic layers: 1) the accessibility layer, 2) the application layer, and 3) the infrastructure layer.

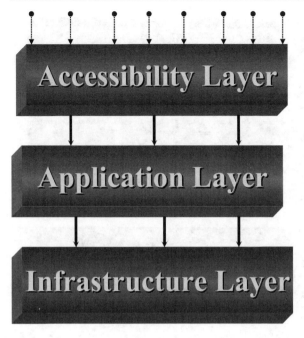

The *Accessibility* layer is the level at which access to data is controlled. Examples include access via the Web; restricted access from a specific machine; or different access levels based on security for various stakeholders such as external partner firms that need access to the enterprise data. This could be termed the *data access or the process layer*.

The *Application* layer is the level at which we view all applications used by the function to ensure smooth operation of the department or entity. Examples at this layer could be the document management system, the reporting system, or the design systems. This could be termed the *data flow layer*.

The *Infrastructure* layer consists of base-level system components that are required in order to build any application. Examples of infrastructure activities would be ensuring that necessary telecom and Internet lines are in place; confirming that you have the proper computer with the appropriate bandwidth to enable your application to work correctly; or the migration from one version of Microsoft Office to another. This could be termed the *technology layer*.

Figure 8. 7 Architecture Layers

❑   There are various technologies and activities that reside beneath each layer. To simplify the layers and better communicate with stakeholders, the IT strategist at Shadow Corporation segmented the architectural view so they could easily understand the drill down to the architecture. **Figure 8.8** is an example of the architectural view.

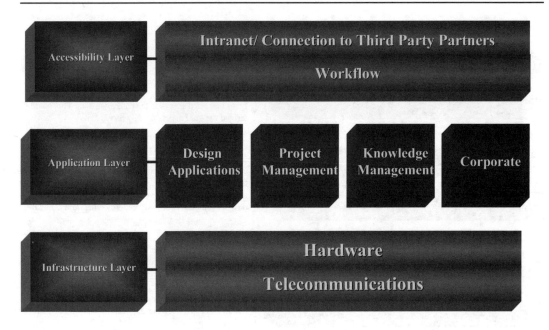

Figure 8. 8   Engineering Entity – Architectural View

❑   Here we see that the accessibility layers consist of Intranet, Internet, and
    workflow technologies. We also see that within this entity, the application
    consists of various applications used by the function to carry out the work
    of its business partners. In addition, the infrastructure layer consists of
    hardware-specific applications and telecommunications equipment. Once
    those components are clearly defined, the next step is to define over time
    the progress that will be made from an IT standpoint. The key is to
    document the progression and the evolution of the IT futures. The
    strategist at Shadow Corporation determined they would like to perform a
    multi-year plan that covers the years 20x1 through 20x3. The architecture
    is therefore tied into the planning time span and must show the progress of
    technology and systems implementation. **Figure 8.9.** is an example of that
    progression at Shadow Corporation:

20x1 SHADOW CORPORATION ENGINEERING INFORMATION SYSTEM ARCHITECTURE

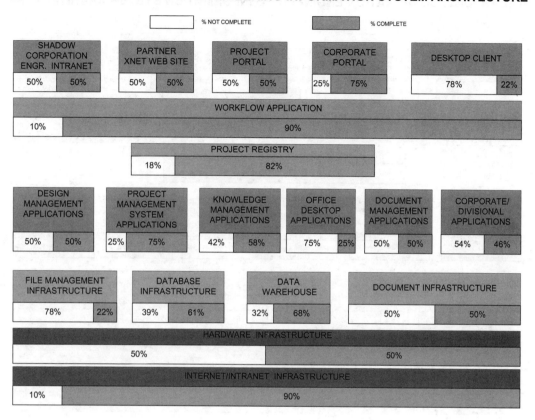

Figure 8. 9 20x1 Shadow Corporation Engineering Information System Architecture

20x2 SHADOW CORPORATION ENGINEERING INFORMATION SYSTEM ARCHITECTURE

| % NOT COMPLETE | % COMPLETE |

SHADOW CORPORATION ENGR. INTRANET	PARTNER XNET WEB SITE	PROJECT PORTAL	CORPORATE PORTAL	DESKTOP CLIENT
50% 50%	33% 67%	33% 67%	25% 75%	39% 61%

WORKFLOW APPLICATION
6% 94%

PROJECT MASTERY
15% 85%

DESIGN MANAGEMENT APPLICATIONS	PROJECT MANAGEMENT SYSTEM APPLICATIONS	KNOWLEDGE MANAGEMENT APPLICATIONS	OFFICE DESKTOP APPLICATIONS	DOCUMENT MANAGEMENT APPLICATIONS	CORPORATE/ DIVISIONAL APPLICATIONS
23% 77%	25% 75%	35% 65%	75% 25%	41% 59%	42% 58%

FILE MANAGEMENT INFRASTRUCTURE	DATABASE INFRASTRUCTURE	DATA WAREHOUSE	DOCUMENT INFRASTRUCTURE
24% 76%	25% 75%	25% 75%	25% 75%

HARDWARE INFRASTRUCTURE
30% 70%

INTERNET/INTRANET INFRASTRUCTURE
5% 95%

Figure 8. 10 20x2 Shadow Corporation Engineering Information System Architecture

20x3 SHADOW CORPORATION ENGINEERING INFORMATION SYSTEM ARCHITECTURE

	% NOT COMPLETE		% COMPLETE

SHADOW CORP ENGR. INTRANET	PARTNER XNET WEB SITE	PROJECT PORTAL	CORPORATE PORTAL	DESKTOP CLIENT
21% 79%	25% 75%	25% 75%	33% 67%	17% 83%

WORKFLOW APPLICATION
2% 98%

PROJECT MASTERY
8% 92%

DESIGN MANAGEMENT APPLICATIONS	PROJECT MANAGEMENT SYSTEM APPLICATIONS	KNOWLEDGE MANAGEMENT APPLICATIONS	OFFICE DESKTOP APPLICATIONS	DOCUMENT MANAGEMENT APPLICATIONS	CORPORATE/ DIVISIONAL APPLICATIONS
23% 77%	23% 77%	23% 77%	27% 73%	32% 68%	31% 69%

FILE MANAGEMENT INFRASTRUCTURE	DATABASE INFRASTRUCTURE	DATA WAREHOUSE	DOCUMENT INFRASTRUCTURE
18% 82%	25% 75%	25% 75%	11% 89%

HARDWARE INFRASTRUCTURE
5% 95%

INTERNET/INTRANET INFRASTRUCTURE
10% 90%

Figure 8. 11 20x3 Shadow Corporation Engineering Information System Architecture

❑ As we see in the architecture picture, the top-level three layers are broken down into their structural components. These components are then assigned percentages based on the perceived and projected investment in each of the architectural component areas. There will be large investments in hardware infrastructure, moving the percentage completion of the hardware infrastructure layer from 50 percent to 95 percent in terms of completion of the vision. The workflow showed limited movement over time due to the near completion of that layer, but we also see that the connection to Shadow Corporation's external partners is expected to be 75% complete by 20x3.

In certain cases, the IT strategist might determine that it is best to communicate the architecture picture in a manner prescribed by Spewak in *Enterprise Architecture Planning*. At other times the strategist might show the progression of the architecture over time by showing the actual infrastructure (as seen in the example to follow). Again, it is important to note that the method chosen to show the migration of technology to technology and architecture to architecture is left up to the strategist. Though we need to use principles such as Spewak's, the communication of the information is equal, if not more important, that the architecture itself.

Bringing the Section Together

In this section we have covered the alignment activities of the business strategy to the IT strategy to the actual initiative. In order to formulate the complete initiative planning agenda, we must also derive the list of potential initiatives on a three- to four-year time span. We can then look at the overall architecture and determine, based on business input, the best progression path to the ultimate vision.

A comprehensive example of the Initiative Planning Section of Business Systems Planning follows:

Initiatives Planning

Table 8. 9 Strategic Business Technology Alignment

IT Strategies	Business Objectives									
	Assure compliance with Safety Regulatoin	Communicate Safety Information	Improve Safety Performance	Provide Readily Access Information at Fingertip	Improve Timeliness of Audits	Limit Losses and Liability	Proactive Working with Associations	Objective 8	Objective 9	TOTAL
Provide mechanism for information to internal & external customers	3	1	3	3	0	2	2			14
Ensure system long & short term going concern issues are addressed	3	0	3	3	0	1	0			10
Evaluate and provide alternatives for efficient business information storage via document management and scanning facilites	2	2	0	2	2	0	0			8
Evaluate systems architecture and provide solutions for current/on-going Business systems	2	2	1	0	2	2	0			9
Provide agenda for IT related training for application and new systems upgrade	2	2	2	2	2	2	2			14
TOTAL	12	7	9	10	6	7	4			

Business Objective Legend

1 ~ Low impact to business objective   2 ~ Medium impact to business objective   3 ~ High impact to business objective

Table 8. 10 Strategic IT Alignment

Initiatives	Information Exchange	Long/Short Term Going Concern	New System Technology	System Integration	IT Related Training				TOTAL
	Information Technology Strategies								
Year 2000 Evaluation	3	3	3	3	3				15
Patent, Trademark, Agreement Systems Module	3	3	3	3	1				13
Forms Contract	3	0	3	2	0				8
TOTAL	9	6	9	8	4				

IT Strategies Legend

1 ~ Low impact to IT strategy   2 ~ Medium impact to IT strategy   3 ~ High impact to IT strategy

Table 8. 11 Strategic Business Alignment

Initiatives	Perform Legal Services	Work with Business Units	Ensure Skills and Resources	Prevantative Law Agenda	Manage Corporate Records				TOTAL
	Business Objectives								
Year 2000 Evaluation	3	3	3	3	3				15
Patent, Trademark, Agreement Systems Modules	1	1	1	0	3				6
Forms Contract	3	3	3	3					12
Total	7	7	7	6	6				

Business Objective Legend

1 ~ Low impact to business objective   2 ~ Medium impact to business objective   3 ~ High impact to business objective

Pictorial View – Three-Year Plan

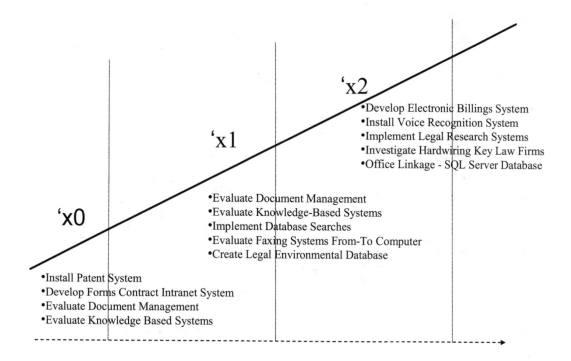

Figure 8. 12   Pictorial View – Three-Year Plan

Architecture Diagram

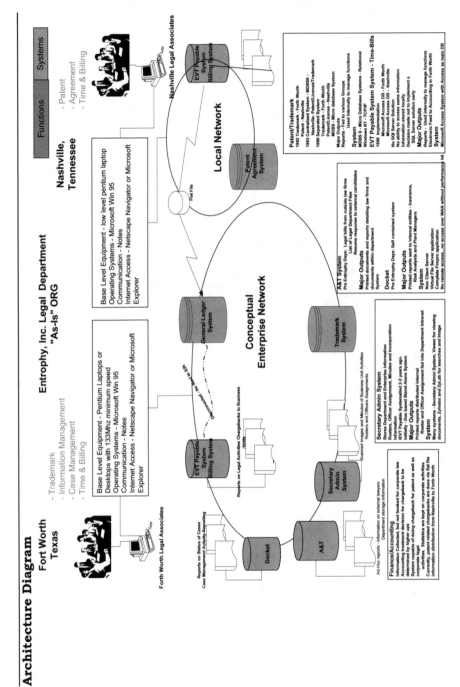

Figure 8. 13 Architecture Diagram – "As-Is" ORG

142

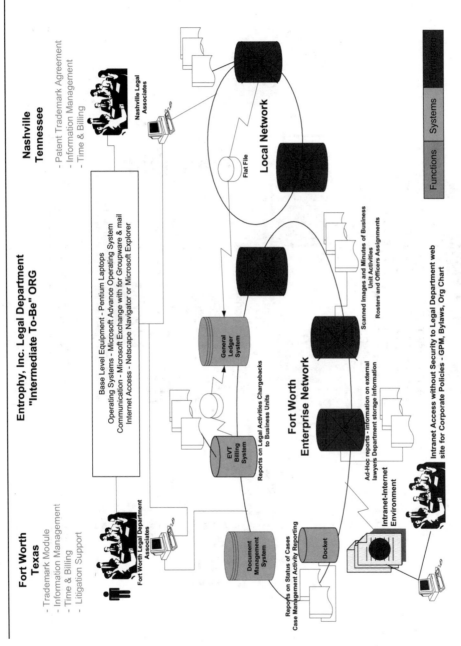

Fort Worth Texas

- Trademark Module
- Information Management
- Time & Billing
- Litigation Support

Fort Worth Legal Department Associates

Entrophy, Inc. Legal Department "Intermediate To-Be" ORG

Base Level Equipment - Pentium Laptops
Operating Systems - Microsoft Advance Operating System
Communication - Microsoft Exchange with for Groupware & mail
Internet Access - Netscape Navigator or Microsoft Explorer

Nashville Tennessee

- Patent Trademark Agreement
- Information Management
- Time & Billing

Nashville Legal Associates

Local Network

Flat File

General Ledger System

EVT Billing System

Reports on Legal Activities Chargebacks to Business Units

Fort Worth Enterprise Network

Scanned Images and Minutes of Business Unit Activities
Rosters and Officers Assignments

Document Management System

Reports on Status of Cases
Case Management Activity Reporting

Docket

Intranet-Internet Environment

Ad-Hoc reports - information on external lawyers Department storage information

Intranet Access without Security to Legal Department web site for Corporate Policies - GPM, Bylaws, Org Chart

Functions | Systems | Eliminator

Figure 8. 14   Architecture Diagram – "Intermediate To-Be" ORG

143

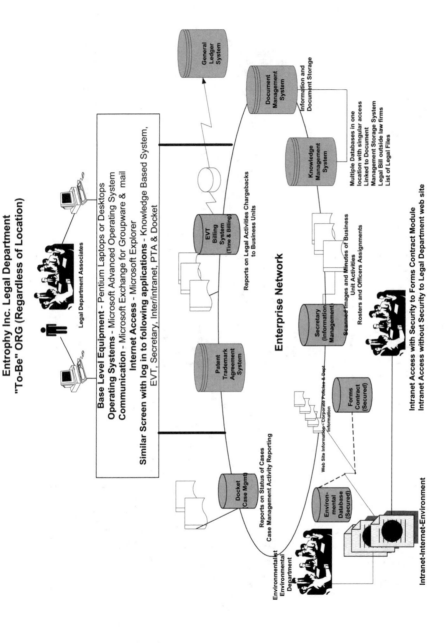

Figure 8. 15   Architecture Diagram – "To-Be" ORG (Regardless of Location)

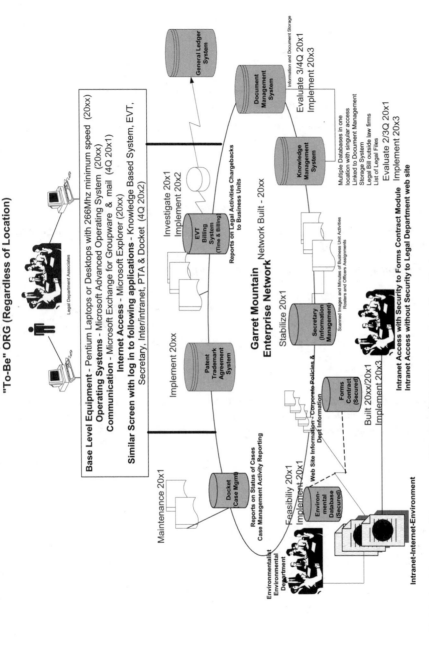

Figure 8. 16 Architecture Diagram – "To-Be" ORG Implementation Date

Questions to Ponder

1. *Is there consistency between the three-year plan and the overall architecture plan outlined in the Entrophy example?*

2. *The implementation of various applications will require changes to the desktop environment and to its underlying infrastructure. What are the possible environment and infrastructure implications?*

3. *Why did Entrophy's legal department decide to eliminate applications from Nashville, Tennessee?*

4. *What are the possible implications, if any, to eliminating applications from Nashville?*

5. *How has Entrophy's desktop environment changed from 1999 to 2003?*

6. *What are the possible strategic and objective drivers for implementing a patent, trademark and agreement system?*

7. *What are Entrophy's most important technology drivers?*

Suggested Reading:
> *An excellent book on the subject of IT architecture is Enterprise Architecture Planning by Steven Spewak, which describes in depth the activities and thought processes that should be used when designing an appropriate IT architecture for an organization.*

9   *Key Tactical Initiatives*

During this part of the strategic plan capture, the IT strategist will delve into the tactical realm of the plan. The purpose here is to elaborate and work out the finer details of the strategy as it relates to specific initiatives. The intent under this information capture is two-fold: 1) clearly define each initiative for the upcoming year and 2) provide analytical information to give qualitative and quantitative justification for the initiative.

The content of this strategic capture consists of:

1) The Key Initiative List and Categorization
2) A Pictorial View: One-Year Plan
3) Key Initiative Description
4) Strategic Theme Analysis.

This section will begin the summarization, and in some cases, the detailed analysis and description of specific projects to be undertaken by the IT function.

❑ **Key Initiative List and Categorization**

Here, we introduce a new term: *"High-Level Detail," or HLD.* High-Level Detail is information that the CEO, CIO, senior executives, or senior IT personnel need to look at across the landscape of activities to see the list of projects for the coming year. It not only documents the lists of projects, but it also delves into related activities such as the technologies to be used and the people associated with the projects.

Specifically, the key initiative list and categorization documents: 1) projects, 2) business justification 3) technologies associated with the projects, 4) scheduled delivery dates for the projects, 5) average full-time and part-time individuals dedicated to the project, and 6) funds allocated for each project.

Projects: The list of projects is a list of initiatives that have been compiled and agreed to by both the business and the IT function for the coming year. It should consist of all tactical projects and the beginning of some strategic projects that will stretch across a one-year time line.

Business Justification: There are many reasons why projects are performed, but there are two fundamental reasons why they are done: 1) strategic necessity and 2) return on investment (ROI).

The strategic necessity basically means that a certain technology move or a paradigm shift is occurring in the industry, necessitating that the organization invest in technology to ensure competitive equality with its competition.

There might be specific ROI reasons for the project, but the focus here is not on specific quantitative reasoning of the project; instead, the reason why the investment needs to be done void of a proper ROI justification.

The strategic necessity reasoning could cover areas such as increased regulatory or compliance pressures that cause the entity to invest in technology. Another strategic necessity justification is the Internet's impact on society—in order to retain customers, a business has to invest in specific technologies to give the client access to their information on the Web.

Speed is the key. There is a need to move swiftly and not take into consideration the specific quantitative benefits of the system. Return on investment justification can be as wide and diverse as possible. The ROI details why a project is being done and shows its benefits. Some examples of these justifications: increased revenue, decreased cost, increased quality, operational necessity, increased level of decision support, and increased customer service.

Important Technologies: The importance of capturing the specific technologies associated with a project is that they enhance the HLD and give the senior executive a clearer picture of the technologies that will be used. This also gives the senior executive a quick scope of the type of technology: client server or desktop; call center or voice response system; massively parallel processing or Glyph; data mining or data visualization technologies. If information is captured along this line, the senior executive can quickly assess the level of investment in new and old technologies.

Schedule Estimates: The focus here is on the timing of the delivery of a particular project. Again, at the HLD level the senior executive can quickly attain how soon a project will be done. A key component of the schedule estimate is to force the strategist to make a best-or worse-case scenario presentation of when the project will be done. This helps the senior executive measure the certainty window that might be available for a particular project.

For example, in order for Insurance Company X to get better information to its sales agents in the field, it develops a project called "PDA Field Launch." The purpose of the project is to deliver small personal computers to sales agents which they can use to download client information. This project supports the business objective of capturing more shares of the marketplace in the upcoming quarter or during the following year. The IT strategist needs to document when the project will be done so senior business executives have an idea whether they will be able to reach their goals.

Full-Time Equivalents: In this case the IT function needs to understand the ramification of the development of projects. The important analysis activity is to determine if there are adequate resources available to do the project in-house. Does there need to be further dedication of resources outside the particular entity? We will call resources outside the entity "consultants."

Estimated Allocation: If we take the projects and the required full-time equivalent, we can quickly determine: 1) if the amount of allocated funds is enough, 2) if any projects need to be eliminated, or 3) if we need additional funds to ensure that all the projects are completed.

The purpose of the *Estimated/Allocated Capture* is to determine the cost of the project and what amount of funds have already been appropriated for the project. The difference between what is appropriated and the total cost of the project is the shortfall required amount.

Table 9.1 J.C. Fitzgerald Financial

Initiatives	Increase Revenue	Decrease Cost	Increased Quality	Increased Compliance/Control	Enable Business Strategy	Operational Necessity	Increased Decision Support	Increased Customer Service	Image	Workflow	Data Warehousing	Voice Response Units	Call Center Technology	Internet Technologies	MPP Large Scale Computing	Electronic Commerce	Wireless Communication	Computer Telephony	New Devl. Methodologies	Best Case	Worst Case	Full-Time Employees	Consultants	Total Project	2001 Estimated	2001 Allocated
	Business Justification								*Important Technologies*											*Schedule Estimates*		*2001 Average Full Time Equivalents*		*$ Estimated / Allocated ($000)*		
JCF Trade - Rollout Ph. II	2	3	2	1	1	1	3	2						X		X			X	2Q00	4Q00	10	0	1,000	1,000	0
Order Entry	1	3	2	1	1	1	1	3						X					X	3Q00	4Q00	15	0	21,250	19,870	0
Phase I Re-Engineered			3	1	1	1	1	1						X					X	4Q00	2Q01	6	0	1,875	1,875	0
Business Edge A/C	3	1	1	2	1	2	1	3	X	X		X	X					X		2Q00	3Q00	0.5	0	750	750	0
Multi-Currency System	2	1	3	1	2	2	1	3		X		X	X	X	X					3Q00	4Q00	4	0	650	63	0
TMD Replacement	1	1	3	3	1	2	3	3		X			X	X	X	X				2Q00	3Q00	4	0	1,500	500	0
Electronic Executions Services	2	3	3	3	3	1	3	1						X		X			X	2Q00	4Q00	4	0	500	500	0
Audit Trail	1	1	3	3	1	1					X									2Q00	2Q00	3	0	500	500	0
OTC - Re-Engineer	1	1	3	1	1	1	1	3		X	X		X	X			X		X	2Q00	3Q00	3.5	0	375	375	0
JCFChoice Target	2	2	3	1	2	1	1	3		X	X		X	X			X		X	2Q00	3Q00	4	0	438	438	0
Mutual Fund Trading System	1	3	3	3	2	1	1	3		X	X		X	X	X		X		X	4Q00	2Q01	7	3	500	500	0
Complete ACATS Rewrite	3	2	3	3	3	1	3							X					X	2Q00	3Q00	5	0	1,250	1,250	0
JCF Registration Workflow	1	2	3	3	3	1				X										3Q00	4Q00	6	0	625	625	0
Compliance Option Monitoring	1	2	3	3	1	1		1		X	X									2Q00	3Q00	4	2	5,230	4,600	0
Total																						76.0	5.0	$36,443	$32,846	$0

150

Table 9. 2 Healthcare United Inc.

Initiatives	Business Justification								Important Technologies											Schedule Estimates		2001 Average Full Time Equivalents		$ Estimated / Allocated ($000)		
	Increase Revenue	Decrease Cost	Increased Quality	Increased Compliance/Control	Enable Business Strategy	Operational Necessity	Increased Decision Support	Increased Customer Service	Image	Workflow	Data Warehousing	Voice Response Units	Call Center Technology	Internet Technologies	MPP Large Scale Computing	Electronic Commerce	Wireless Communication	Computer Telephony	New Devl. Methodologies	Best Case	Worst Case	Full-Time Employees	Consultants	Total Project	2001 Estimated	2001 Allocated
Affiliated Medical Groups		3							X					X		X	X			2Q01	4Q01	9	0	2,001	1,800	1,800
Delegated Provider Program		3	2			2		3		X		X	X	X		X	X	X		3Q01	4Q01	29	27	7,000	6,000	6,000
NOVA Programs		3				2						X	X			X	X	X	X	4Q01	2Q02	20	62	24,000	20,700	20,700
Location Consolidation		1	2	1	1				X	X										2Q01	3Q01	13	8	2,100	1,000	1,000
Underwriting System		2				2														3Q01	4Q01	11	10	4,000	3,000	3,000
Financial Function Enhancements		2		1	2		3													2Q01	3Q01	1	13	2,001	1,000	1,000
Pilot Program				3							X			X						2Q01	4Q01	15	2	5,400	2,001	2,001
HIPAA				3		2														2Q01	2Q01	10	25	25,000	10,400	10,400
PLA Program				3		2														2Q01	3Q01	3	3	600	350	350
MIB Migration Program			2																	2Q01	3Q01	6	5	1,100	600	600
New General Ledger Program																			X	4Q01	2Q02	14	35	7,500	5,000	5,000
Total																						131.0	190.0	$80,702	$51,851	$51,851

Table 9.3   State Street Financial Banking Unit

Initiatives	Increase Revenue	Decrease Cost	Increased Quality	Increased Compliance/Control	Enable Business Strategy	Operational Necessity	Increased Decision Support	Increased Customer Service	Image	Workflow	Data Warehousing	Voice Response Units	Call Center Technology	Internet Technologies	MPP Large Scale Computing	Electronic Commerce	Wireless Communication	Computer Telephony	New Devl. Methodologies	Best Case	Worst Case	Full-Time Employees	Consultants	Total Project	2001 Estimated	2001 Allocated
	Business Justification								Important Technologies											Schedule Estimates		2001 Average Full Time Equivalents		$ Estimated / Allocated ($000)		
Document Imaging	X		X						X										X	3Q00	1Q01	0.3	0.5	182	119	119
Electronic Banking		X	X		X	X		X						X		X				2Q00	4Q00	0.9	1.0	629	289	289
Loan Origination	X	X	X	X	X	X					X	X								1Q00	3Q00	0.3	0.5	594	252	252
Financial Reporting				X	X		X				X									3Q00	4Q00	0.9	3.0	940	681	681
Upgrade Ntwk Backbone					X	X														2Q00	4Q00	0.0	0.0	208	35	35
MVXZ Upgrade															X					2Q00	4Q00	0.0	0.0	120	30	30
Revisioning T4	X	X		X	X				X	X	X	X	X	X				X		4Q00	1Q01	2.0	1.0	307	307	307
Teller Conversion	X	X	X	X	X	X					X									4Q00	2Q01	5.0	1.0	495	495	495
Tax Reporting		X																		2Q00	4Q00	0.1	0.0	62	62	62
EDYMN System Upgrade			X			X							X							4Q00	1Q01	0.0	0.0	550	46	46
Total																						9.5	7.0	$4,087	$2,314	$2,314

152

In the example Table 9.3, State Street Financial's banking unit, $4 million will be invested on its IT initiatives. While the amount of money to be invested is unimportant, what is important is the amount of information captured about its projects. Investment will be made in the bank's infrastructure in terms of its network backbone. The justification for that is due to operational necessity. Overall, the State Street Financial banking unit is investing in such technologies as imagining and data warehousing. Limited funds are being spent on new development technologies and computer telephony. From a quantitative analysis perspective, the unit will require roughly seventeen new hires of staff, and there is an investment gap of about $2 million between the total project cost and what the estimated funds are.

❑ **Pictorial View: One-Year Plan**

In Section 6.2.3 an IT function developed a three-year plan that was agreed upon by their business unit. It captured the initiatives and projects that were expected to be launched by the business unit over a time span of three to four years. Once the alignment activities have been done (Section 6.2.3) and there is agreement on priorities of the projects going forward, the IT function can determine a schedule of activities for the year.

The important item in this information capture is to create and illustrate a two-dimensional picture of activities. On one dimension the time, and on another are the activities. A third dimension that can be painted in the picture is the resource. Resources could be either dollars or people. It is a third unseen dimension that will determine exactly how the picture will be painted and the possible outcomes that could be devised from the schedule of activities.

The outcome of the one-year picture is the immediate agreed upon schedule of activities to be undertaken by the IT function and agreed by business partners. It is a simplistic picture that gives the viewer a look into the IT function at any particular time. It also helps determine which levels of activities are being performed or maintained by the function. One key note is that this one-year picture should be focused more on strategic elements of the plan, rather than on tactical activities. Although its a one-year plan, it should be considered tactical in nature.

Here are some examples:

1998 Systems Strategic Plan - Major Initiatives

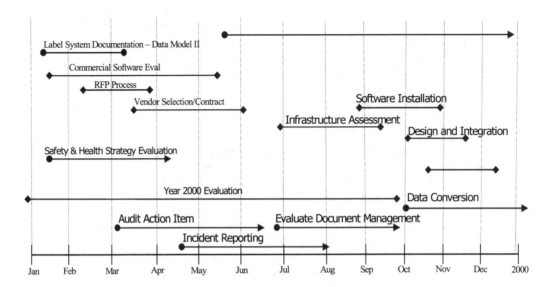

Figure 9. 1 Environmental Service Unit

1998 Systems Strategic Plan - Major Initiatives

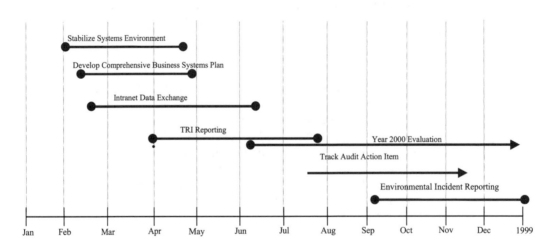

Figure 9. 2 Safety Department

The above example is that of a chemical company's safety department. This picture shows us that the unit is involved in not only evaluation of its overall strategy, but also in plans to implement a few systems such as the audit action items, incident reporting, and evaluation of document management systems. A data model is being created for the labeling systems that could form a possible basis for software installation to occur in September.

Prior to the software installation, an infrastructure assessment will be completed beginning in July and ending right after the software installation. As can be observed, it is clear that the year is 1999 based on the Year 2000 evaluation activities that are occurring for a good portion of the year.

The key to the picture is to give the IT strategy analyst an indication of the projects and workload to be expected throughout the year. It also forms the basis for discussion in and between the IT personnel and the stakeholders who will be involved in the development and eventual rollout of the projects.

❑ **Key Initiative Description.**
The Key Initiative Description (KID) is a detailed description of the particular projects that will be undertaken. The KID consists of relevant and specific information that will be used to help determine the priority of the project relative to the others in the portfolio. The more information that is available for each KID, the more comprehensive the business systems plan will be and the more robust the document will be upon presentation.

Each KID consists of detailed descriptive information of a particular project. It is a natural evolution from the one-year picture in that the one-year picture details all the projects for a particular year. The KID, on the other hand, is prepared for each project that is documented on the one-year picture. The following is a list of information normally captured in the *Key Initiative Description.*

❑ *Key Initiative Name:* Name of the project and/or initiative.
❑ *Description:* A brief description of the overall project and/or initiative, detailing the overall objective and timing of the project.
❑ *Business Purpose:* Identifies the specific business reasons why the project is being undertaken. The project could be undertaken for

process improvement or as a sub-project of an overall call center implementation.

❑ *Initiative Result/Deliverable:* This captures the end result of the project and answers the question: "What will be produced when this project is completed?"

❑ *Initiative Approach:* This is fundamentally tied into the system development approaches of the organization and refers back to the first section of the document. Depending on the system development life cycle methodology, the information captured here is how the project will be developed. If the project involves an off-the-shelf package approach, it could involve a) analysis, b) design, c) installation, d) customization, e) data conversion, f) testing, g) training, h) implementation, and I) post-audit. The key is to capture as much detail as possible.

❑ *Initiative Economics/Staffing & Budget:* This is the ROI *(Return on Investment Value),* the justification and analysis of each project. Analysis must be done on a project-by-project basis of the cost of the project, the relative revenue contribution or savings to be gained, and the expenditure to be made in the current year and future years. These important ingredients will form the basis of any return on investment analysis. An evaluation of the resources, hours per week, number of weeks, company-driven resources versus externally-driven resources, and their associated costs should also be captured.

❑ *Technology Requirement:* The project manager and/or strategist needs to document what technologies are associated with this undertaking. By identifying the technology, an analysis can quickly be made as to the potential for completion. Early adoption of new technologies increases the project's overall risk while usage of tested and known technologies will lower risk.

❑ *Sub-projects*: If an initiative includes one or more projects, it is important to capture those projects here, only by identity. This gives a better understanding of the size and enormity of a project.

❑ *Changes to Ongoing and Non-Discretionary Activities:* This is a project impact analysis. Detail is given, or captured, relative to what the potential changes that will be experienced from the development and implementation of this project.

❑ *Link to Enterprise-Wide Initiative:* Identify, if possible, the known or proposed linkages to other technology undertaking for the current or future years. The capture of this information is good from an analysis perspective in that it helps the strategist and those at a higher level identify the potential intersect points of project that will be developed.

❑ *Initiative Risk Assessment:* Risk assessment provides some detailed questions that will help implementers and stakeholders understand the relative possibilities of the project's successes or potential failure. The risk analysis takes into consideration:

    a. The possibility of scope change. The higher the possibility of scope changing over time, the lower the chances are that the project will be completed on time.

    b. The organizational impact. The higher the favorable impact, the better the chances are that this project will remain a high priority.

    c. Probability of success being measured. An inability to measure potential success begs the question, "Why is initiative being done?"

    d. The regulatory impact. The higher the regulatory impact, the more important it is to push the project out the door.

    e. Emerging technology impact. The higher the reliance is on new and emerging technology, the higher the project risk. The potential for failure on emerging technology initiatives are greater than for those on current technology.

    f. Impact of outsourcing. If the project is being outsourced, project risks increase.

    g. Impact of vendor package. Off-the-shelf packages are usually less risky than custom development. The project risk will be lower, all things remaining constant, if the development underway is an off-the-shelf package that will be developed with limited customization.

    h. Likelihood of *Business Drivers Changing*. If the business driver has the potential for changing over time, the project risk will be increased either due to the potential of scope reduction or scope increase.

Here is an example of a *Key Initiative Description* for a project:

Project Delta
Description
AAPT is a re-engineering initiative consisting of multiple programs that are
transforming the way we do business at the national service centers. Project
AAPT had its inception in February 20xx. 20x2 will be its final implementation
phase. It consisted of first consolidating into the national service centers followed
by implementing programs that move "business-as-usual" toward world-class
standards. Numerous programs are part of AAPT. Some of the key programs
being pursued and consisting of, in part, information technology components are:

Case Set-up and Maintenance
Service Set-up
Service Processes
Financial Support
Provider Network

Business Purpose
The business purposes of the AAPT programs are to reduce costs and to improve
service levels.

Initiative Result/Deliverable
The systems infrastructure to support the healthcare concern's operational
environment will be built. Some new applications will be built; some examples
are a provider contracting workbench, a contracts Publisher, a client data capture
tool, and a plan detail record toolkit. Existing systems will also be enhanced.

Initiative Approach
A structured approach will be followed. Individuals from each unit will be
responsible for creating and/or editing their information that will be uploaded to
the Website.

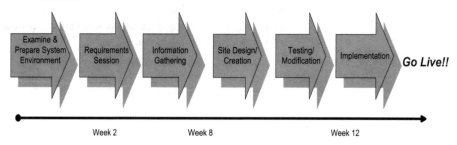

Figure 9. 3   AAPT Initiative Approach

Table 9. 4 AAPT Initiative Approach Description and Time Table

Activities		Time Estimates
I.	Examine & Prepare System Environment • Evaluate current environment • Evaluate infrastructure capability	8 Weeks
II.	Requirements Session • All units input for design • Initial design creation • Assignment of responsible party from each unit	12 Weeks
III.	Information Gathering • Research required information for each unit • Create individualized unit conceptual site • Test conceptual map	13Weeks
IV.	Site Design & Creation • Convert documents to HTML format • Create indexes, search mechanism • Create formatted Web pages, navigation • Test design & created site	10 Weeks
V.	Testing & Modification • Consolidate all site information • Test conceptual design • Test created Website • Modify Website – application	5 Weeks
VI.	Implementation • Create training material • Prepare procedures and processes for ongoing maintenance • Load business unit pages • Install and test hardware and software	9 Weeks

Table 9. 5 AAPT Initiative Economics

Current Year Cost	10,570,000	0
Current Year Revenue Contribution	0	0
Current Year Cost Savings	18,234,000	0
Net	$ 7,664,000.00	$ -
Total Project Cost	0	0
Capital Expenditure		
Current Year Capital Expenditure	7,000,000	0
Total Project Capital Expenditure	9,000,000	0

Table 9. 6 AAPT Initiative Resources

Resource	Hrs/week	# of weeks	Company	Con-sultant	External $	Total Cost
Project Lead (¼ time)	2	15	X			
Business Personnel (½ time)	1	7	X			
One FTE (TBD)	8			X		
½ IT Infrastructure member	N/A	N/A	N/A			

Technology Requirements
Imaging Technologies
Client/Server Development Technologies
Workflow Technologies
Document Management and Desktop Architecture Technologies
Changes to ongoing and Non-Discretionary Activities
Implementation of AAPT Programs will result in significant shifts in the systems support structure.

Links to Enterprise-Wide Initiatives or Centers of Excellence (COEs)
Architecture
Distributed Systems
Initiatives Risk Assessment

Table 9. 7 AAPT Initiatives Risk Assessment

Questions	High	Medium	Low
What is the probability that scope will change over the initiative's duration?	X		
What is the organizational impact of the initiative?	X		
What is the probability of success being measurable?		X	
What is the regulatory impact upon the initiative?			X
What is the emerging technology impact upon the initiative?	X		
What is the impact of outsourcing upon the initiative?	X		
What is the impact of a vendor package upon the initiative?		X	
What is the likelihood of the business drivers changing over the initiative's duration?		X	
What is the initiative's demand of organizational focus and capacity?	X		
To what extent does the initiative require operations and business participation?	X		

Project Imaging

Description
This project is to further expand the bank's image pilot as a comprehensive document image management system that can be scaled for departmental and bank-wide applications. This project will replace a Macintosh-based legacy imaging system. We will be able to leverage experienced corporate resources and provide a shared technology solution through the use of a corporate standard software product (Eastman Software's Open/image and Open/workflow).

Business Purpose
To provide a cost-effective means to image home equity loan documents for the life of the loan with the capability to retrieve documents for viewing. Typically these documents are stored off-site for an extended period and require manual processes to retrieve. This initiative will convert the existing images and database on the MARS imaging system to Open/image to eliminate the use of two imaging systems for the Home Equity Portfolio.

Initiative Result
- ❑ To expand the pilot system installed for cards operations to meet needs of home equity and their requirements to store documents for the life of a loan.
- ❑ To increase volume of documents scanned per minute, decrease response time to three seconds or less to view images, and have ability to print documents.
- ❑ To eliminate need to manually change optical disk volumes to view documents or have to retrieve documents from off-site storage.
- ❑ To archive documents to online storage for short-term retrieval then migrate process to long-term storage.
- ❑ Savings found in initiative stem from more efficient employees and workflow.

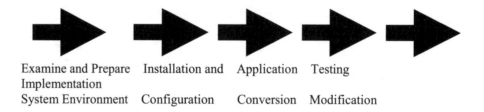

Examine and Prepare	Installation and	Application	Testing
Implementation			
System Environment	Configuration	Conversion	Modification

Figure 9. 4   Project Imaging Initiative Approach

Table 9. 8 Project Imaging Initiative Approach Description and Time Table

	Activities	Time Estimates
I.	Examine & Prepare System Environment	X Weeks
II.	Installation and Configuration	X Weeks
III.	Application Conversion	X Weeks
IV.	Testing & Modification	X Weeks
V.	Implementation	X Weeks

Table 9. 9 Project Imaging Initiative Economics

	Estimated	Allocated
Current Year Cost	119	0
Current Year Revenue Contribution	0	0
Currrent Year Cost Savings	87	0
Net	$ (32)	$ -
Total Project Cost	182	0
Capital Expenditure		
Current Year Capital Expenditure	95	0
Total Project Capital Expenditure	95	0

Technology Requirements
Hardware:
Image Server (1) HP LHPro 6/200 Model 1-Array (Unit w/ 32MB)
Scan Stations (2) Windows '95
Viewing Stations (5) Windows Advanced Operating System
Scanners (2)

Software:
Open/image
Windows NT XP or Advanced Operating System
Arc serve Tape Backup
Windows Advanced Operating System
MS SQL Client Access

Sub-projects

Expand existing Open/image systems for home equity.
Convert Macintosh-based TRAT systems to Open/image

Links to enterprise-wide initiatives
Image/Workflow

Table 9. 10 Project Imaging Initiatives Risk Assessment

Questions	H	M	L
What is the probability that scope will change over duration of the initiative?		X	
What is the organizational impact of the initiative?			X
What is the probability of success being measurable?	X		
What is the regulatory impact upon the initiative?			X
What is the emerging technology impact upon the initiative?	X		
What is the impact of outsourcing upon the initiative?			X
What is the impact of a vendor package upon the initiative?	X		
What is the likelihood of the business drivers changing over the initiative's duration?		X	
What is the initiative's demand of organizational focus and capacity?		X	
To what extent does initiative require operations and business participation?	X		

Not all information is required during the development of the plan; additional information will be gathered over time. As you can see from the imaging project, the detail as to how they will approach the project from a methodology standpoint is missing. Before the project is kicked off or during the project planning stage of this project, the specific information about approach will be finalized.

❑ **Strategic Themes**

The *Strategic Theme* is simply an analytical tool. This tool is used by senior strategists and analytical personnel to analyze the impact of a unit's technology effort as it relates to the importance of the business objectives. There are three components to the *Strategic Theme*: 1) business themes, 2) technology initiatives, and 3) selection criteria.

Business themes are usually business-related activities that detail the direction and importance of the initiatives relative to the business. They are usually devised and formulated by senior business strategic functional staff. Business themes are normally major business segments that senior management considers to be important to the organization. If they are important to the organization, they must have some linkages to the technology projects and initiatives that will be developed. They could be in the area of sales and marketing, customer recognition, information advantage, infrastructure and/or technology innovation.

Sales and Marketing themes could be based on contacting the customers (contact management), analyzing information about the customers (information analytics), and tracking sales (sales tracking).

Touching the Customer themes has activities based on electronic interaction with the customer and reaching the customer directly in their homes (householding).

Information Advantage themes have to do with gathering information about the customer and analyzing the information that will ensure competitive advantage. Activities specific to information advantage are the collecting of massive data about the customer (data ware housing), analyzing data to formulate information (mining and visualization), and the quality and delivery of information (quality and delivery).

Infrastructure includes those activities at the base level of the IT development. As Section 6.2.3 outlines, these activities deal with desktop technology upgrades, massively processing systems, and processing environment.

Technology innovation could be a mainstay of the organization. The innovation could be based on image and workflow activities to reduce the paper build-up in an organization; electronic commerce and electronic business for Web development; voice recognition to increase customer service or data warehousing for in-depth customer analysis and segmentation. The level of technology innovation will depend on the industry and the organization's technology capability and intent, whether the organization is a technology follower or a technology advancer.

The initiative will be documented, and the strategist based on analysis of the information collected in the KID, will determine how important or how relevant each initiative is to the themes of the organization.

The key point to the Strategic Theme is that the technology initiatives, which are undertaken, are linked specifically to the themes (CEO's intent) of the overall organization. This is not just an alignment link, but more of a linkage of the themes to initiatives.

The following **Tables 9.11, 9.12 and 9.13** are examples of strategic themes for particular organizations.

Table 9. 11 Investment Arm of Major Financial Services Firm

Initiatives	Sales and Marketing			Touching the Customer		Information Advantage				Infrastructure								Technology Innovation			
	Contact Management	Information Analytics	Sales Tracking	Electronic Interaction	House-holding	Ware-housing	Quality	Delivery	Mining	Desktop Technology Upgrades	Major Increases in Processing Power Communications or DASD	Shift from One Processing Environment to Another	Image	Workflow	Data Warehousing	Voice Response Units	Call Center Technology	Internet/Intranet	MPP Large Scale Computing	Electronic Commerce	Wireless Communications
Recordkeeping	X			X		X	X	X	X			X	X	X		X		X			
Transfer Agency	X			X		X	X	X	X				X	X		X		X			
Trade Management					X	X	X	X	X			X				X		X			
Annuities	X			X		X	X	X	X			X	X	X		X		X			
Common Front End				X		X	X	X	X			X	X	X		X	X	X		X	
Call Center				X		X	X	X	X			X					X				
Cash Control				X		X	X	X	X			X						X			
Plan Accounting	X			X		X		X	X			X									
Security Master		X				X	X		X			X									
Portfolio Accounting						X	X	X	X			X									
Reporting							X	X	X	X		X									
Real Estate				X		X		X	X	X		X									
Vision		X				X		X	X	X		X									
Compliance Expert System		X				X		X	X	X		X									
Standard Desktop									X	X		X									

Table 9.12 Healthcare Concerns

Initiatives	Sales and Marketing			Touching the Customer			Information Advantage			Infrastructure								Technology Innovation			
	Contact Management	Information Analytics	Sales Tracking	Electronic Interaction	House-holding	Ware-housing	Quality	Delivery	Mining	Desktop Technology Upgrades	Major Increases in Processing Power Communications or DASD	Shift from One Processing Environment to Another	Image	Workflow	Data Warehousing	Voice Response Units	Call Center Technology	Internet/Intranet	MPP Large Scale Computing	Electronic Commerce	Wireless Communications
Affiliated Medical Groups												X						X		X	X
Delegated Provider Program				X	X			X			X	X				X	X	X		X	
AART Programs										X	X	X	X	X	X	X	X	X		X	
Consolidation Program						X	X	X		X											
Underwriting Desktop		X				X				X	X	X									
Treasury Function Enhancements							X	X				X			X						
Client & Member Internet Access Project				X														X			
ITLS System																					
PITA Program							X	X			X				X						
NRL Migration Program							X	X													
New General Ledger Program							X	X	X	X											

Table 9. 13 Soverntry National Bank

Initiatives	Sales and Marketing			Touching the Customer		Information Advantage				Infrastructure			Technology Innovation								
	Contact Management	Information Analytics	Sales Tracking	Electronic Interaction	House-holding	Ware-housing	Quality	Delivery	Mining	Desktop Technology Upgrades	Major Increases in Processing Power Communications or DASD	Shift from One Processing Environment to Another	Image	Workflow	Data Warehousing	Voice Response Units	Call Center Technology	Internet/Intranet	MPP Large Scale Computing	Electronic Commerce	Wireless Communications
Imaging													X								
Electronic Banking				X														X		X	
Home Equity Loan Orig.						X	X	X	X					X							
Fin. Report Sys. Re-eng.						X	X	X	X						X						
Upgrade Ntwk Backbone							X														
Telecom CMS Upgrade														X	X	X	X				
ADP Conversion		X			X	X	X	X	X			X		X	X	X	X				
Deposits Tax Reporting					X	X		X													
DirectDial				X						X							X				

Assume that all of the previous examples were business units of a major financial company. Can a CIO look across the landscape of all IT initiatives and identify to the CEO the intent of their technology organization and explain how IT will help the CEO achieve his/her goal? By rolling up the *Strategic Theme* for each of the businesses, the CIO will be able to do that. Therefore, when completed and rolled up to the CIO level, plays an extremely important role in detailing to senior business management the value to be gained from IT initiatives and projects. This can be seen in the above examples.

Bringing the Section Together

We have discussed in detail the evaluation and capture of the key initiative list, the one-year plan, elements of the initiative, and the strategic themes. Once all that information is collected, it provides valuable information and analytics on the condition and direction of the IT function. This information also gives senior management valuable intelligence on the state of IT within the company and its business units. An example of the intelligence capture is listed on the next page for the Safety and Health function of a medium-sized chemical company.

Table 9. 14 Key Initiative List and Categorization

Initiatives	Business Justification								Important Technologies											Schedule Estimates		2001 Average Full Time Equivalents		$ Estimated / Allocated ($000)		
	Increase Revenue	Decrease Cost	Increased Quality	Increased Compliance/Control	Enable Business Strategy	Operational Necessity	Increased Decision Support	Increased Customer Service	Image	Workflow	Data Warehousing	Voice Response Units	Call Center Technology	Internet Technologies	MPP Large Scale Computing	Electronic Commerce	Wireless Communication	Computer Telephony	New Devl. Methodologies	Best Case	Worst Case	Full-Time Employees	Consultants	Total Project	2001 Estimated	2001 Allocated
Incident Reporting							X	X											X	2Q99	4Q99	2	2	100,000	100,000	0
Audit Action Items			X	X			X	X			X								X	2Q99	4Q99	1	0	200,000	200,000	0
Document Management			X	X		X	X	X											X	4Q99	1Q00	2	2	400,000	400,000	0
REG INFO Initiatives			X																	1Q99	4Q99	1	0	100,000	100,000	0
Safety and Environmental Strategy Assessment			X	X		X		X												1Q99	1Q99	1	2	0	0	0
Toxicology and Product Regulatory Compliance (TPRC)			X				X	X						X						1Q99	2Q99	1.5	2	500,000	500,000	0
Software (MNTR System)			X				X	X		X				X					X	4Q99	4Q99	2	1	400,000	400,000	0
System Implementation			X						X					X					X	4Q99	1Q00	2	2	635,000	635,000	0
Data Conversion - MSDS			X						X	X				X					X	4Q99	2Q00	2	3	175,000	175,000	0
Training							1	3												4Q99	4Q99	1	0	15,000	15,000	0
Total																						15.5	14.0	$2,525,000	$2,525,000	$0

Pictorial View – One-Year Plan

1998 Systems Strategic Plan - Major Initiatives

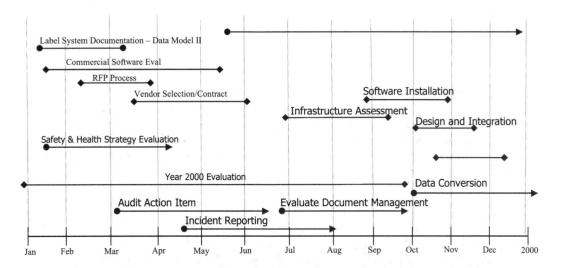

Figure 9. 5 Pictorial View – One Year Plan

Key Initiative

Commercial Software Evaluation - MNTR
Description

This initiative will present a methodology for the evaluation and identification of a tool to replace the current MNTR system. This initiative will not devise or present a selected vendor, but will demonstrate that effective evaluation and analysis of the product was performed.

Business Purpose

By performing an evaluation of available software to replace the MNTR system, we will be able to "by the end of the day" say that a proper product was chosen as the likely successor to the system. From a business standpoint, we will be able to: 1) assure compliance with manufacturer safety/product regulations, 2) communicate product safety information more effectively and efficiently, and 3) provide internal customers with readily accessible regulatory and pertinent technical information.   The enterprise is focusing on growing the business, but proper analysis has to be done to ensure that the underlying systems currently in place will be able to maintain or enhance the ever-changing business environment.

Initiative Result/Deliverables

No new system will be built.

Initiative Approach

A structured approach will be followed that includes examination of overall MNTR system. This should be a secondary process to the data model. Once the analysis and evaluation phases are completed, we will be empowered with the necessary information to make the decision to replace the system or enhance the current one.

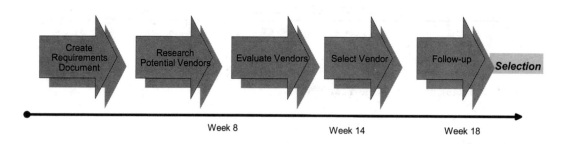

Figure 9. 6   MNTR Initiative Approach

Table 9. 15 MNTR Initiative Approach Description and Time Table

Activities	Time Estimates
Create Requirements Document Develop requirements checklist Develop case scenario (optional)	4 Weeks
Research Potential Vendors Develop vendor 'long list' Conduct phone interviews/review marketing material Develop vendor 'short list'	4 Weeks
Evaluate Vendors Conduct demonstrations/site visits	8 Weeks

Obtain third-party opinion Issue RFP (optional)/fill out requirements checklist	
Select Vendors List and weigh top vendor selection criteria Score short list vendors Select preferred vendor	2 Weeks
Follow-up Address requirements non-compliance issues Commence contact negotiations	2 Weeks

Table 9. 16 MNTR Initiative Economics/Staffing & Budget

Insert the initiative economics in the table below and briefly state staffing and budget information.

	Estimated	Allocated
Current Year Cost	25,000	0
Current Year Revenue Contribution	0	0
Currrent Year Cost Savings	0	0
Net	$ (25,000)	$ -
Total Project Cost	0	0
Capital Expenditure		
Current Year Capital Expenditure	0	0
Total Project Captial Expenditure	0	0

      The project should include joint participation between Safety & Health and IT personnel. Budget for the effort will be determined from a detailed project plan taking into consideration the availability of company's resources and time needed to complete the effort. A table is attached for this effort.

Table 9. 17 MNTR Initiative Resources

Resource	Hrs/ Week	# of Weeks	Company	Consulta nt	External $	Total Cost
Project Lead (¼ time)	3	18	X			
S&H Personnel (½ time)	3	18	X			
FTE	10	3		X		25000

Technology Requirements

No technology implication determined.

Sub-projects
No sub-projects to this initiative.

Changes to ongoing and Non-Discretionary Activities
There will be no change to ongoing and non-discretionary activities based on these initiatives.

Links to enterprise-wide initiatives
No linkage to other enterprise initiatives.

Table 9. 18 MNTR Initiatives Risk Assessment

Questions	High	Medium	Low
What is the probability that scope will change over the initiative's duration?			X
What is the organizational impact of the initiative?	X		
What is the probability of success being measurable?			X
What is the regulatory impact upon the initiative?	X		
What is the emerging technology impact upon the initiative?	X		
What is the impact of outsourcing upon the initiative?			X
What is the impact of a vendor package upon the initiative?	X		
What is the likelihood of the business drivers changing over the initiative's duration?			X
To what extent does the initiative require operations and business participation?		X	

Table 9.19 Strategic Themes

Initiatives	Sales and Marketing			Touching the Customer		Information Advantage				Infrastructure			Technology Innovation								
	Contact Management	Information Analytics	Sales Tracking	Electronic Interaction	House-holding	Ware-housing	Quality	Delivery	Mining	Desktop Technology Upgrades	Major Increases in Processing Power Communications or DASD	Shift from One Processing Environment to Another	Image	Workflow	Data Warehousing	Voice Response Units	Call Center Technology	Internet/Intranet	MPP Large Scale Computing	Electronic Commerce	Wireless Communications
Incident Reporting		X			X					X											
Audit Action Items					X										X						
Document Management					X																
REGSCAN Initiatives																					
Safety and Environmental Strategy Assessment		X					X	X													
Toxicology and Product Regulatory Compliance (TPRC)																					
Software (MNTR System)					X					X			X	X				X			
System Implementation					X					X			X					X			
Data Conversion - MNTR		X					X	X										X			
Training																					

Questions to Ponder

1. *What is the total investment expected for this Safety and Health Unit?*

2. *What key themes will the CEO focus on?*

3. *Define clearly how the IT entity of the Safety and Health Unit will be addressing the issues of the company?*

4. *How long is the Commercial Software development cycle for this project?*

5. *Are there any technology initiatives from the Safety and Health standpoint to address the customers of the company? Why?*

10   *The IT Organization and Strategies*

The focus now shifts and we will focus completely and directly on the IT organization. In previous sections we focused on the business unit—its strategies, goals, objectives, and processes. We focused on the needs of the business and the important technology initiatives that could be developed to enable the business to achieve success. We focused on the alignment and linkages of business objectives to IT strategies. We have gone so far as to link these IT strategies to initiatives and ultimately back to the business objectives.

All of those activities are paramount to the realization of the business's goals and objectives. However, from an IT management perspective, equally and more important is the IT landscape that is available to develop new systems, maintain current systems, develop new processes and ensure alignment of technology strategy to business activities. These are detailed parts of the puzzle that must be addressed from a strategic standpoint in any strategic capture to ensure adequate execution of the plan. The components of the strategic capture that form the basis of the IT Landscape are as follows:

a.   Operational Goals
   - The People
   - The Processes
   - The Technology

b.   Common Technology

c.   Enterprise-Wide Technology Efforts

d.   Shared Technology Solutions
   - Outsourcing
   - Infrastructure
   - Emerging Technology Investigations
   - Applications

e.   Non-Standard Technology

f.   First Time Use of Technology

g.   Vendor Solutions

- **Operational Goals:** This strategic capture will focus on the IT organization. It paints the picture of where the organization is and how much progress is expected during the year along the dimensions of a) people, b) process and c) technology.

Organizations attack this from various levels. Some take reactive approaches by developing their organizations relative to the projects that they must undertake now and in the future. Others attack it with a proactive approach by focusing on the organization's culture in absence of all the projects. The proactive approach generally yielded a greater return because the focus is not on the projects, but more on the environment in which the projects will be developed.

There are three components of the *Operational Goals*: people, process, and technology.

1.) *People* are the most important component in IT development— or any other development for that matter. From a strategic standpoint there must be adequately trained personnel resources with the capability to undertake the work that must be completed. Some IT organizations fall short because they do not focus on training their employees to understand the latest technologies in the marketplace. Once there is this degradation, there will be a decrease in the level of service available to offer to the customer. Once there is a decrease in customer service, then like anything else, the customer will look elsewhere. There is a direct connection to the training and the level of expertise that resides within an IT organization to its level of customer retention and customer satisfaction.

2) *Process* is equally important. In some organizations there isn't a concrete understanding of the processes used for system development. Instead there is a focus on product and service delivery. The Software Engineering Institute has defined various levels at which an organization should operate as it relates to the documentation and the understanding of the technology processes at a firm. A great majority of the organization is at the lowest level on the SEI scale primarily due to a lack of focus on processes and documentation.

3) *Technology*. Organizations need to have in place a technology roadmap or a schedule of technology activities to ensure business success. This roadmap is a communication document that is critical to the understanding and direction of the IT group relative to new and old technologies. Some firms have made a fundamental decision to be technology followers, while some have made a strategic decision to focus on being a cutting-edge company. There

is nothing wrong with either decision. What's important is that each organization examines its industry and makes a decision that doesn't hinder it from achieving its business goals.

Whether it is people, process, or technology, the IT landscape must address them in full. It is done not only as a means of external communication, but as direction setting for information technology personnel.

Examples of *Operational Goals* capture are as follows:

MTAC Enterprises

Operational Goals

People

      Currently, legal department support from an IT perspective is limited at best. The current position of IT strategist has been filled. Over time, as the department begins to focus more on strategic initiatives and less on legacy systems, there will be a need for additional support personnel. Support for the following maintenance systems will be needed: *Master Data System, Secretariat Information System, Docket System and the Legal Department Intranet site*. The focus in 20xx will be on replacement of the *Intellectual Property System* and additional Intranet applications.

Processes

      Major projects under consideration in 20xx: replacement of the *Patent, Trademark and Agreement System*; contract online to access all of MTAC's associates with updated forms; *Document Management* as a major initiative; and development of a *Legal Environmental Database*. The primary purpose of these initiatives is to improve current processes involve with legal documentation and retrieval. Most systems implemented will be package software. It is the hope that MTAC will not get into the application development businesses. A concrete methodology will be used as it relates to the acquisition of package software. In cases where time and effort outweigh the detail methodology, a well thought-out approach will be used focusing on time, planning, and dollar expenditure.

Technology

      See architecture diagram in *Initiative Planning Section*.

Gemini Safety and Health Service Unit

Operational Goals

      The organization currently depends on external consultants to perform most, if not all, of system-related activities at Gemini. The issue to be dealt with is that of organization knowledge and transfer. The more dependent we are on consultants, the less likely it is that information will stay in the organization. For the moment, resources dedicated to IT efforts on the environmental front are limited to the consultants and one IT individual in the Safety and Health Unit.

People

Currently only one permanent resource is dedicated to the IT effort of safety and health. In addition, there is a chemist with a good background in IT who performed some IT-related tasks for the unit. Currently there are two consultants on call who have dedicated their effort to getting the LABEL system in use and stabilized.

Processes

The development process here is grounded in the *Product Life Cycle* effort. Projects and initiatives are scoped out via a planning session after which projects are given appropriate budgetary clearance before development is undertaken. Development is performed now with the use of internal IT infrastructure profession who provide systems guidance and other IT knowledgeable chemists.

Technology

The unit will follow the standards set in place by the corporate IT function. Deviation is allowed only when there is a proven business justification and need. Currently, the major IT initiative is the stabilization and function of the LABEL system. That application is written with rapid application development software called MAGIC; information is stored in a BTRIEVE database. The application is under evaluation via data models and commercial software evaluation for possible replacement. If this route is chosen, it will be accomplished in 20xx.

Other technologies in use include TSCAN CD-ROMs that store regulatory state and in addition to Gemini's proprietary information. There are also limited scanning activities that take place. Scanning and document management initiatives have been placed in favor of an enterprise approach that takes into consideration the needs of the various service group's from Finance, HR to Legal Department.

Processes

Elmer Corporation Systems will be world class by YExx. The Software Engineering Institute's Capability Maturity Model provides a world-class standard to measure by. With the SEI's model as guidance Elmer Systems has implemented the following processes:

- SQA Process Definition and Training
- Software Configuration and Management
- Project Management Definition and Training
- Project Tracking and Oversight Definition and Training
- Sub-Contractor Management Training
- Requirements Management Definition

Adherence to these processes will create a World-Class system community that produces high-quality solutions to business requirements, quickly and cost-effectively.

How do you know if you are world-class? The answer lies in Metrics. Elmer Systems will employ measurement processes to assure our world-class performance. Key measurements are as follows:

- CIO Key Performance Measures
- Benchmarking with Peer IT Companies
- Continued SEI Assessments and Process Improvements

❑ **Common Technologies:** The purpose of the common technology capture is to gather information as it relates to common technologies used for development within a particular year. This is a summarized view of the overall technology undertaking, not in terms of a direction or roadmap, but more in terms of a list of project-based technologies.

Examples of common technology capture are:

❑ Initiative will be driven by the need to have Internet technology and client server solutions as it relates to information access. No specifics have been defined as it relates to the type of database technology. Due to the scale of the organization, most database development work will be done in Microsoft Access, which is one of corporate enterprise standards.

❑ Technologies employed in the initiatives are compliant with the Enterprise Standards. The list is as follows:
- Microsoft Advanced Operating Systems
- Image & Workflow
- Internet/Intranet
- Warehousing
- Call Center Technology
- Voice Response Units
- MPP Large Scale Computing
- New Development Methodologies

❑ **Enterprise-Wide Technology Effort:** Any stakeholder or IT strategist, at the business unit or corporate level, would like to know what other technology-related activities are ongoing in the enterprise. The reason for this understanding is to:
  ❑ Share within one particular unit the undertaking at the enterprise level;
  ❑ Form the basis for excellent information analysis when rolled up at the corporate level;
  ❑ Serve as a means of consolidating and re-directing projects that would otherwise be developed in duplicative forms across the enterprise;
  ❑ Cuse a business unit to slow down its effort, if other entities within the corporation are ahead of them in terms of development.

The capture of the enterprise-wide technology effort can also be used as a communication vehicle to business partners so they understand their requests are part of a bigger effort and could be developed or deployed by other major efforts within the corporation.

Example of the *Enterprise-Wide Technology Effort*:

A partnership with the Enterprise-wide technology efforts exists in every aspect of the insurance system's technology deployment. These efforts include an across-the-board roll-out of PDAs to sales agent and other relevant parties in the Insurance unit.

❑ **Shared Technology Solutions:** This capture consists of activities related to outsourcing, infrastructure, emerging technologies investigations, and applications. Understanding this information gives management keen insight into the possible savings to be gained from outsourcing activities or third-party activities (TPA). The quantity of these TPAs when rolled at the enterprise level gives clear indication as to the dollar resource and expenditure dedicated to the effort. A good knowledge and understanding of emerging technology efforts will help the technology unit understand the possible risks and gaps that exist with the implementation of new initiatives.

Example of *Shared Technology Solutions*:

MTAC Corporation
Possible Shared Technology Solutions
None.

Outsourcing
No process or function available for outsourcing.

Infrastructure
There is a need to implement Groupware solution. The enterprise does not have a universal standard for the support of e-mail. This issue will be addressed later. For the interim, the Intranet serves as a viable solution that roughly 70-80 percent of the organization currently has access.

Emerging Technology Investigations
No emerging technology investigation undertaken in the Unit. That is being commissioned and done by the corporate IT function.

Applications
None.

Healthcare of Americas
Possible Shared Technology Solutions
None.

Outsourcing
IBM Global Services
Symmetric

Infrastructure
Notes deployment and VM elimination.

Emerging technology investigations
CORBA technology.

Applications
None

❑ **Non-Standard Technology:** It is of extreme importance that there is adequate capture of non-standard technologies within any organization. In most plans, non-standard technology is not captured. There has to be adequate trust involved especially for business units to inform corporate that they are using non-standard technology. From a pure academic and conceptual standpoint, it is an excellent idea to capture this information because business units might be using the same type of non-standard technology that, when rolled up and evaluated, makes perfect sense in addressing business needs. However, it is the release and capture of this information that appears to be difficult because business units tend to be less than forthcoming about the use of non-standard technologies.

Example of Non-Standard Technology:

> *Synergistic Bank*
> The Bank is not currently planning to deploy any non-standard solutions as part of a BSP initiative. We will continue to maintain existing non-standard technologies, such as the Mac desktop and Oracle databases, as part of our BAU activities.

❑ **First-Time Use of Technology:** The capture of first-time use of technology lends itself to the risk assessment of the entire portfolio of a technology group. If the intent is to use first-time technology on most of the group's technology undertaking, the risk assessment will be relatively high. This information has to be communicated to business counterparts so there is adequate understanding and leveling of expectation related to use of emerging and first-time-use technologies. First-time use of technologies could give indications of the possible risks associated with completion or non-completion of a project.

Example of First-Time Use of Technology:

> *Synergistic Bank*
> The use of Internet Banking software tools as specified within this BSP will represent the first use of this technology at the bank. Though it is being used as a relatively new technology, due to the training effort that has been expended this year, we approach this first-time use with relatively lowered risk assessment. Our people are ready for the use of this technology.

❑ **Vendor Solutions:** Some technology groups have as their operating principle to focus on technology development utilizing third-party vendors and not to focus on in-house technology development. The use of vendors to implement solutions has been a win-win for many organizations. The roll-up of vendor solution information gives senior officers a clear understanding of the amount of funds being expended on vendor solution. If the dollars being spent on vendor solutions is high, the potential for moving from vendor solutions to absolute outsourcing might be the next logical step. Vendor solution, in and of itself for the purpose of a technology unit, is not that important. However, what is important is how many vendor solutions there are and across what landscape these vendor solutions exist. Awareness of this is significant intelligence for senior business and IT managers.

Example of First-Time Use of Technology:

Healthcare of Americas
Symmetrics is being used to build the *Client Data Capture Tool* described under the NOVA Program. On another program it is the intent of this technology unit to utilize NSL systems for the deployment of our patient tracking Web-based information. NSL will be utilizing technologies that are first-time use within Healthcare, but it is a program that we believe can be managed with adequate supervision and communication.

Bringing the Section Together

This capture focuses on the IT organization, its people, process and technology and the various activities it performs to position and complete initiatives and projects driven from the business.   The key to this section capture is true honesty about the level and the number of resources and their capability relative to the direction of the business. Here is one example:

Operational Goals

People

IT organization at Synergistic Investments is composed of *Business Systems, Network Operations, Client Services, Disaster Recovery and Telecommunications.* The staff depth and level of competency is currently quite high. As Synergistic Investments migrates away from Macintosh as its dominant desktop and toward NT, there will be some dilution of expertise, but we plan to mitigate this through training.

In mid-20xx, Synergistic Investments handed over day-to-day telecommunications operations to CTS with their staff matrixed into the Synergistic Investment's Systems Executive. This arrangement has worked well and resulted in significantly lower costs associated with telecommunications staff. The CTS organization has not yet evolved to be able to support *Interactive Voice Response* (IVR) systems, and this activity is currently performed by local contractors under CTS direction.

As part of the general reorganization around functions the opportunity was taken to establish an O&S framework at Synergistic Investments. An O&S executive was named and an effort was undertaken to better align systems responsibilities with the systems executive and IT organization. As a result there were several systems functions identified at Synergistic Investments that were not controlled by the IT area. In 20x1 work will be undertaken to migrate these functions over to IT.

Processes

Synergistic Investments currently employs an in-house application development/program initiation process called SDM, *System Development Methodology.* The SDM process has been reviewed against emerging corporate methodology and found to be largely consistent with it. In 20xx Synergistic Investment's SDM process was modified and fully consistent with corporate guidelines.

At Synergistic Investments today there is no formal IT resource allocation process aside from the BSP and annual budget process. In 20xx a Systems Council was formed at Synergistic Investments to address this issue.

Technology

Synergistic Investments' core application processing operations have been outsourced to third parties. These third parties provide deposit, general ledger, credit card, trust and other lending functions. Synergistic Investments' technology architecture is three-tiered: desktop, transport, and application. Some applications are locally resident, such as decision support systems and cost allocation systems, while others reside at the TPA level. We have found this architecture to be flexible and scalable.

Synergistic Investments' technology infrastructure evolved over a period of ten years with little involvement from the corporate technology area and as a result any current "standards compliant" systems are more a result of parallel evolution rather than integrated planning.

Synergistic Investments is making significant efforts toward a compliant infrastructure in the following ways:

- All newly-purchased computer hardware is acquired through POPS and is standards compliant.
- Synergistic Investments will be converting to corporate IP Addressing scheme.
- Synergistic Investments has adopted the policies and standards set forth by Corporate.
- Synergistic Investments will be formulating a plan to adopt Sybase as the DBMS of choice on a go-forward basis.
- Lotus Notes was the e-mail standard at Synergistic Investments in late 1997/early 1998.

Common Technologies

The attributes common to the initiatives are as follows:

- Projects will be controlled employing a standard development methodology.
- Applications employing desktop computers are being deployed under Win NT.
- Any in-house developed applications employing RDBMS are SQL compliant.

- All application systems are network based. There are no free-standing technology islands being developed.
- All new applications developed, purchased or outsourced will be Y2K compliant.

Enterprise-Wide Technology Efforts

The following are Synergistic Investments' BSP linkages (initiatives or other items contained within the narrative) to Excellence Centers or Corporate initiatives:

Image Workflow
Internet
Architecture
Data Management
Data Mining
Project Management
Call Center

Possible Shared Technology Solutions

None identified at this time.

Outsourcing

Synergistic Investments employs the following third-party systems:

Total Systems: Credit Card, Home Equity, OPL
M&I Data Services: Deposits, Lending, General Ledger, AP
SunGard: Trust

Synergistic Investments has used TPAs for core data processing applications for over eight years.

Infrastructure

Not applicable.

Emerging Technology Investigations

Synergistic Investments is currently evaluating Internet Synergistic banking application tool sets such as Edify and Microsoft's Marble product. This is discussed further in our Internet Synergistic Investments' initiative.

In 20xx Synergistic Investments had leveraged the Imaging/Workflow COE by piloting Open/image. The pilot was expanded to include home equity documents in 20xx. See the *Loan Origination* initiative for more information.

Applications

None noted at this time.

Non-Standard Technology

Synergistic Investments is not currently planning to deploy any non-standard solutions as part of a BSP initiative. We will continue to maintain existing non-standard technologies, such as the Mac desktop and Oracle databases, as part of our BAU activities.

First-Time Use of Technology

Internet Synergistic banking software tools as specified within this BSP represents first-time use of this technology at Synergistic Investments.

Vendor Solutions

As noted earlier within this BSP, Synergistic Investments depends heavily on third-party processors for core data processing. Initiatives that are dependent on TPAs include CD tax reporting and the upgrade to TS2. Neither of these initiatives represents first-time use of a particular vendor and will be managed as normal business items with them.

In this case, Synergistic Bank gives a clear and detailed account of its people, processes, and technology. It further defines how any potential "Achilles heel" might hinder the bank from achieving its purpose.

Questions to Ponder

1. *What is a potential "Achilles heel" for Synergistic Investments in terms of execution of its strategies?*

2. *Define clearly the potential impact of outsourcing for Synergistic Investments?*

3. *Is IT group focusing on any new or emerging technologies?*

4. *Is there any risk associated with first-time use and emerging technology across a technology group?*

5. *Why is it necessary to share information about the use of non-standard technology? Why isn't it?*

Potential Strategic Initiatives

The potential strategic initiatives are a list of initiatives that could have made the list of current year development initiatives, but were not able to due to resource restraints. The importance of highlighting these initiatives is that they form the basis for excellent discussions between senior business and IT executives as they relate to 1) understanding of the state of resources, and 2) whether the portfolio of projects needs to be re-optimized.

Listing potential strategic initiatives usually takes place once the four-year portfolio of projects is developed. Once the one-year calendar of projects is developed, there might be projects that could have met the one-year cycle, but due to resource restraints, they are moved off the table for the following year.

The re-optimization might require additional funds or the elimination or re-directing of current or future projects. The process to re-direct or eliminate funds would require the business and technology executives to come to an understanding of not only what will be eliminated, but also the potential impacts of the elimination and re-direction.

Fostering and re-directing can occur during formal presentation sessions with business executives or it can be done during the plan development stage. The ultimate driver for the dialogues is to develop discussion as it relates to potential benefits from delaying or diverting projects from the current year to future years. During the discussion, projects that were once off the table might potential be brought back for the current year due to re-directing of resources—both people and funds.

Potential strategic initiatives entails listing initiatives and projects in table form followed by descriptive definition of the project as outlined in **Chapter 9.** The only difference in the descriptive form is that less information is needed. Information required is: 1) initiative/project name, 2) description, 3) business purpose, 4) initiative result, and 5) impact and alternatives.

Information collected here is the same as that in **Chapter 9** with the exception of *impact and alternatives*. Here, the strategist will document the potential impacts of executing on the project or choosing not too. Alternatives could be that the business might fall behind the competition if a project is not done. Or, risk of delay could be too great in the eyes of the strategist, and they must highlight the potential analysis to their business partners.

Bringing the Section Together

The capture of this section is not enormous. Instead, the purpose here is to capture the initiative that would pose a potential risk to the business if they were not executed on. The example below focuses on the J. Johnson Insurance Company.

Table 10. 1 J. Johnson Insurance Company

Initiatives	Required Resources		$ Estimated ($000)
	Full-Time Employees	Consultants	Total Project
Desktop Migration to NT	0	2	1,901
Risk Management Systems	1	3	2,500
	0	0	0
	0	0	0
Total	**1**	**5**	**$4,401**

Desktop Migration to NT

Description

J. Johnson banking unit's desktop technology infrastructure is not compliant with overall cooperate IT standards. In an effort to standardize company-wide on a common suite of technologies, the bank plans to migrate from a Macintosh-based desktop computing platform to the Windows NT enterprise computing environment. This initiative was categorized as a "potential" initiative because of the bank's current financial position. This initiative would result in the write-off of existing desktop computers.

Business Purpose

By adopting enterprise standardized computing systems, the unit will be able to leverage corporate resources to help achieve reduced acquisition and support costs. It will also create a more simplified computing environment, improve operating system availability, and provide greater inter-operability.

Initiative Result

Desktop migration from Macintosh to PC: Transition all internal computer systems, applications, and functions from Macintosh computer system to Windows advanced operating system. This includes converting in-house developed applications to the advanced operating system.

Impact and Alternatives

The most practical alternative is the tactical deployment of Windows NT as hardware is replaced or as business issues warrant it. This alternative is embedded in the BSP initiative. If we do not migrate, we will continue to operate in a dual platform environment, which complicates training, information sharing, and leads to inefficiencies in the technology support function.

Risk Management Systems

Description

Currently, risk management processes for the calculation and aggregation of all components of financial risk are performed using spreadsheet documents. This initiative entails the design, development, and implementation of a new systems architecture and software solution for these risk management processes.

Business Purpose

Financial risk management

Initiative Result

The technical recommendation is the first part of the initiative and has been deferred.

Impact and Alternatives

Describe impacts if initiatives are not pursued in the coming year, either qualitatively or quantitatively. The process will continue as usual with spreadsheet documents. This is a cumbersome solution to the problem at hand, but given the cost and relative low payback quantitative value to be gained from the initiative, it is best to delay.

J. Johnson's Insurance Unit technology strategist concluded that two projects fit the profile of a potential strategic initiative that didn't make the list of current projects. The focus in this example is on the *impact and alternatives*. Clearly it can be seen that had the $1.9 million been available, the desktop migration from Macintosh environment to a PC environment would have been possible. Alternatively, there could have been good reasoning for deferring the initiative for another year.

In this situation, the cost-benefit and risk-reward analysis must be done to evaluate whether a technology initiative should go forward. Technology and business executives must make the decision to remain on an older platform if the payoff for waiting is greater than the investment to be made.

CASE 3 Jack Weidemeir – Kingsfield Financial Capital

Before joining the ranks at Kingsfield Financial, Jack worked at First Society Savings Bank in its information technology department. His primary responsibility at First Society was human resources and payroll systems. He managed four employees and was responsible for Benefits Applications upgrades and new releases.

Jack arrived at Kingsfield in May, during a period where the company was undergoing the transformation and spin-off from ADL Corporation. Jack's role at Kingsfield was to get human resources and payroll's benefits systems up and running on an AS-400 system called Feefdum.

During his first month, Jack's approach to his new job was from a managerial standpoint. The IT department was able to make decisions to get things done in an expeditious manner. Its director, Roger Ward, had been in charge of the department at corporate headquarters, which consisted of about sixty people. Jack believed the IT department was not truly global and instead focused on systems within corporate that extended out, in a limited manner, to some of the business units.

Since the spinoff, Roger had been focusing on local systems and had not yet established global responsibility in terms of extending IT's scope to reach within the business units. Jack recalled that he was not clear as to how the organization was structured. The AS-400 systems were implemented globally, but the role of corporate IT in terms of leadership and standard setting was unclear and not up-to-speed. Although the business units appeared to have autonomy, Roger influenced the decision to implement systems globally with the CEO and business owners.

Jack saw "resistance from all sites to the corporate technology direction. The company struggled with what direction IT should follow, centralization versus decentralization. He remembered that Roger made some strategic systems decisions. Roger would personally choose the system, implement it locally and had a tendency to dictate to everyone else within the business and service units.

Jack reported to Nigel Ford in charge of system applications and thought he was a good manager. One realization that most employees at Kingsfield had at the time was that they all thought of themselves as part of the big conglomerate, ADL, rather than the expected swift and nimble Kingsfield.

At ADL, the IT department was considered an island that didn't respond efficiently and effectively to its customers. This led most users to not count on IT, but to seek help from external consulting firms or to do it themselves. The customers had a non-reliant view of the IT department.

Jack found himself wondering why he ever came to Kingsfield. The place seemed engulfed in no support for IT, fighting between the groups, and dictatorial relationship of IT with the business. He decided that either everything would explode or that something very good would come from all the challenges.

Management Change

Executive management was receiving more reports about the decline in working relationships between IT and the rest of the business. Meetings between the CEO and Roger echoed that it was time for a change. Roger's response was that the business was uncooperative—not his department.

Not only did he refuse make changes, but the more he was told of the deterioration, the more he became entrenched in his belief as to where the problem was. The CEO asked Roger to leave in December—a year-and-a-half into Jack's tenure. Reaction from IT was mixed—some thought it was for the best, but no one knew the actual reason why Roger was let go.

There were speculations about his professional conduct and the systems he had implemented. The fact that various IT leaders did not agree with Roger's dismissal was a concern for the CEO. But, he felt the poor customer service permeated deep into the organization. Shortly after Roger's departure, some of his lieutenants also left the firm. It was Jack's view that there was direct correlation between the departures of the IT executives and the increase in IT customer satisfaction. Jack felt there was now more open communication between IT and the business.

New Management

At the previous organization, Nigel Ford and Roger Ward were in charge of the application division and Richard Ferguson oversaw operations. For the time being, until a new head of IT was named, Nigel and Richard were heading up all the systems. Both men knew there was a need for drastic changes and time to be cooperative with the business. They also thought that instead of thinking tactically, it was time to focus on strategies that could enable the business.

Eighteen months after Roger's dismissal, the IT department organized its first-ever off-site IT gathering to discuss strategies. The CEO attended and discussed issues he thought affected IT and how they could be addressed. He also explained why Roger had been released. The CEO stated that they needed new direction and that it was time to turn the ship around. He said the primary goal of the firm since its spin-off from ADL was to get its own system. Roger had been given that task and had accomplished it. However, in doing so, he had allowed everything else to fall, including focusing on other issues relevant to the business and ensuring that other maintenance systems were operational.

Management noticed the decline in customer support. The CEO had been told that IT needed to focus on servicing the business and told the group he was deeply considering outsourcing.

Needless to say, most of the participants at the meeting were stunned. Shortly thereafter, numerous IT workers resigned. Jack was disappointed and figured his job was on the chopping block. He began a passive job search because he believed that if he was allowed to stay on the ship as it was maneuvered in a new direction, it would be good for his career.

Nigel informed him of a newly created *business technology liaison* position that would be solely responsible for servicing the HR business function at Kingsfield. Jack stopped his search and told Nigel he was interested. He prepared himself for the new position by reading books and speaking to industry colleagues who performed similar duties at other companies.

New Leadership

Six months later, Calvin Birmingham was hired as Kingsfield's new vice president of information technology. Calvin was hired to shake up the organization and to fix the customer service problems that existed at Kingsfield.

Calvin came highly recommended and had a strategic background. From what Jack knew, he had ideas about methodologies to put in place in order to help the organization achieve a higher standard of service. Jack's first meeting with him was impressive. Calvin seemed down to earth, fair, and forward thinking. He was not concerned about past history and was more interested in what tactics and strategies he could put in place to make things better. He even expressed concern for Jack's personal career goals.

Jack had a lot of questions for Calvin about his position. He wanted to know how it was defined, who he would report to, and the best way to execute it. Although Jack thought he was capable of handling his new position, he was uncertain and believed it was not defined correctly. He didn't see big differences from his current role of supporting HR to his role of creating strategies and implementing systems for the function. He thought it only brought him closer to the managerial function of the job more so than the technical. After much thought, he concluded he was comfortable with the position and wanted to pursue a path forward. He knew what strategic partnership meant, but he was unsure of how to get there.

Three other business technology liaison positions had been filled at Kingsfield besides the one that Jack had filled. The four associates met to discuss what strategic partnership was, and from this came strategies on how to become a partner and to create the *Business Systems Plan*.

One of the associates, Frank Callitran, introduced the concept to the group. He had used it at a previous firm and thought it served as the foundation for all IT activities executed at the firm. He explained how it had become an extremely important part of the job. There was a set process to BSP. The key point Jack remembered Frank echoing was that the BSP was a good process, but how it is executed is up to each IT liaison.

Business Strategy Process

One of the keys to the *Business Systems Plan* is that there must be a clear understanding of the business. There must be a clear understanding of the strategies and objectives of the unit. Where is it going? What are its strengths? What are its weaknesses? In what competitive environment does it operate? What are the various business opportunities that exist in the company's industry?

At Calvin's advice, Jack contacted AON Enterprise, a strategic consulting firm. AON's strength was that it could help companies define their technology, infrastructure, direction, and strategy.

The following year, from April to August, the human resources' process service areas were surveyed throughout all sites and businesses, both locally and globally, to gather information such as objectives, processes, business missions, goals, etc. The focus was specifically on the process service areas. Prior to AON's initiative, the entire HR Department had gotten together to define the overall HR strategy. This did not change one year later. The work that AON did was to complement the HR strategy that was defined the year before.

High-level steps involved in the process were:

- Survey the process service areas.
- Discover the business vision and direction.
- Review the current architecture—locally and globally.
- Utilize the HR Strategy formulated the year before to further define the overall IT strategy.
- Complement with the HR Business Strategy from the prior year.
- Create presentation that highlights the direction of IT, the complementing IT Strategy and the expected direction of the unit from an HR perspective.

- As a result of the union with AON, a draft of the HR/IT Strategy and benchmark was completed.

During the information gathering process, Jack felt like a "participant" rather than a leader. He saw it as his "education" because he had never worked on global assignments before and AON was working to define strategies and direction from a global perspective. He found it to be an interesting and extremely impressive process and thought it was good enough to be executed on.

One interesting reaction from the business units was that they were tired of information gathering. They wanted to see action. The sites were tired of IT gathering information and leaving. Jack knew that even though they did not see the big picture of this, it was worth undertaking.

There were numerous worldwide initiatives that were defined as a result of the AON investigation. Jack knew he had the background and experience to create the *Business Systems Plan*. In preparation he would take the information from the AON HR/IT report review and process it for the business systems plan.

Jack took the following steps to ensure success:

1. Gathered information from the AON HR/IT strategy;
2. Met with senior HR personnel to explain the BSP Process;
3. Met with Process Owners to explain the BSP Process;
4. Took sheets from the BSP that outlined the business objectives and asked the owners for possible initiatives that might enhance the process;
5. Worksheets were sent to the business partners for them to give additional initiatives that they wanted;
6. Jack linked the initiatives from HR/IT strategy to *Strategic Alignment Matrix in BSP;*.
7. Initiatives were linked to the business objectives and then to the IT strategies using the *Strategic Business Technology Alignment*.

Met with Senior HR Personnel to Explain the BSP Process

Jack met with Greg Barnes and Millard Anderson, senior executives of the HR function. He explained the process, which was unclear to them. The process was new and the learning curve was huge for Greg and Millard. Jack was unsure of some of the process steps and felt like a novice at putting together the BSP. He did not have a formal document to show Greg and Millard and instead used the table of contents to show them what he was trying to accomplish.

Here is the table of contents he used:

Table of Contents

His next step was to meet with the business process owners to gather the information.

Meeting with the Process Owners

Jack then met with six process owners in one-on-one sessions to discuss the procedure. No formal documents were used to map out the plans. Instead, Jack started with a worksheet and business plan index. He met with Greg Barnes, who was in charge of HR, Millard Anderson of Benefits, Nell Williams of Global Training, Crimson Tailor of Remote Training, Jane McDonnell of Medical, and Ronald Willacks of Compensation.

All of them were generally supportive of parts of the strategy. Jack thought that some grasped the concept behind it at the time, but some were just happy that he appeared to know what was going on. Nell Williams appeared to be very supportive, as she had an agenda and utilized the process to include it.

Millard seemed to understand well what was going on. Crimson was supportive although he did not thoroughly understand it. Jane was inquisitive, asking numerous questions because the process was new to her.

One repeated comment Jack gathered from these meetings was that his role was not clearly defined to people nor was it defined to his direct reports. It was confusing to the process owners who had previously viewed Jack as a tactician, and what he was now explaining was high-level strategy.

Jack took all the information he received from the various process owners and tied it back to the specific business objectives that were identified in the AON/IT strategy document, which was now the strategy section of the BSP.

Create Presentation That Highlights Initiative

Jack created a draft of the document that included all the initiatives that had been developed and defined from all the process owners. The documents included four initiatives from each process owner. Jack felt that the twenty-four initiatives were too much, but knew that if he brought it to Greg Barnes and Millard Anderson they would be able to prioritize it for him.

Finalization and Prioritization

Jack used an unorthodox approach to the finalization of his BSP. He did not follow the standard process of reviewing it with all involved in the process. Instead, he reviewed it with the head of the unit and his second lieutenant. The process steps were as follows:

- The prioritization meeting was held with Greg and Millard (Priority Setting Committee). There was no review of initiative prioritization with direct reports.

- Greg did not grasp the idea at all. Jack realized that Greg should have seen the process earlier and had it explained in clear detail.
- Greg and Millard reviewed all the projects and decided unilaterally to cut fifteen of the initiatives.
- Jack was told to communicate what got cut to the process owners.
- He left the meeting feeling disappointed because he was now caught in the middle of the Priority Setting Committee and the actual process owners.
- When he communicated the cuts to each of the process owners, he was blamed for failing to gain approval for the projects.

Lessons Learned
- Jack felt like he was being criticized and later attributed to a lack of communication between the committee and the actual process owners.
- He realized he was still considered the applications manager and not the strategic partner, which he had expected.
- The actual process owners expected him to do the tactical work while at the same time perform strategic duties.
- He did not have the staff or the budget to perform both.
- He opposed to the Priority Setting Committee from cutting some of the projects. By resisting, he ultimately took on accountability for the projects instead of the actual process owners.

In retrospect, Jack learned a lot from the process. He did not believe it was successful. Instead:

1) He admits it would have been a good idea to get all the process owners together in a room with the Priority Setting Committee. This would have avoided all the miscommunication that served as one of the primary impediments to the BSP process.

2) He felt if he had more knowledge of the process, he would have been able to take command of various situations as they got out of hand.

3) He felt that his role was not clearly defined, and this became confusing for the customers he supported.

4) He believed top management should have explained the process clearly to their counterparts on the business side and that would have trickled down throughout the organization, which in turn would have helped his cause tremendously with the process owners.

5) He knew that new leadership was an excellent idea and one that he embraced. It was something that was good for Kingsfield. He felt he was not ready for the next iteration of the BSP. He learned his lesson well that year. Experience is costly, but it helped him to grow.

The Business Systems Planning Process

As we examine planning from a budgeting standpoint, we can also analyze planning and its relationship to the Information Technology investment. The diagram on page 207 gives us a pictorial view of Information Technology and business activities that are involved in the planning cycle. The diagram shows the linkage points and the overlap between business and IT. It also demonstrates the understanding of the business environment in which the IT entity of any corporation operates and support.

The Business Systems Planning (BSP) process is not separate from the business process. We must clearly delineate the difference between the business planning activities and the business systems planning activities. Both processes occur simultaneously.

In previous chapters, we examined the business planning process. We looked at the detail of the activities occurring within the process and how they create a viable plan. The process used to create the plan is formal, but this is required to ensure that the various businesses of an organization understand and can clearly state their goals, missions, and objectives.

The business planning process is not separate from the activities on the technology side. The key is to ensure that the development process is occurring on a somewhat parallel track. It does not mean that both occur simultaneously—they can be a few months apart, but one process should not be completed before the other begins.

In the following section we will review the business process to help gain a better understanding of how to proceed with IT planning. We will examine the processes at the higher level and delve into sections of the process in detail. The higher level involves strategy development, initiative development, budget authorization, and actual implementation. It shows the overall process steps involve in each of the high-level overarching processes. But, it also contains detail steps to be taken to meet the overall higher level main focus of each process levels. It is important for the reader to keep in mind the big picture as we delve into the specific process steps within the technology planning arena.

11   *Business to Information Technology View*

The Information Technology process is the most important element of the overall IT strategy formulation. It forms the basis of how the technology function will perform and how it will interact with the business. It also will define the expectations of the business and of the IT functions. Plus, it will prioritize the activities to be performed over a fixed period of time.

The Business-to-Information Technology view details over a timeline the activities that should be performed to ensure adequate completion of not only a Business Systems Plan, but also a Business Plan. The hope at the end of the process is for members of the IT department and members on the business side to clearly understand the direction of the corporation as it relates to technology undertaking and its alignment with the business.

It is important for the reader to refer to the diagram on page 195 as you read this chapter. Every company and corporation needs a formal process for planning their business undertaking. An IT department is no different. It must have a formal process to help justify and prioritize the activities to be undertaken.

Our diagram shows the process divided into business and technology activities. Ideally, any business strives to understand its environment and to determine its strategies, initiatives, objectives, goals, and the drivers needed to address particular business issues.

From an IT perspective, once the business call is made for new initiatives to be formulated, the IT function should be developing its own initiatives. The IT initiatives are not developed independently, but in concert with the business unit.

The IT function must partner with the business to understand the intent of the business and to develop specific projects that can address the need of the business. The IT function's initiatives will drive the business to achieve the goals set forth in its strategy development.   In order to develop the initiatives, the function must also partner with the business to ensure there is adequate and proper understanding of the business. This will also ensure that the strategy of the business is in line with the strategy, objectives, and initiatives of the IT function.

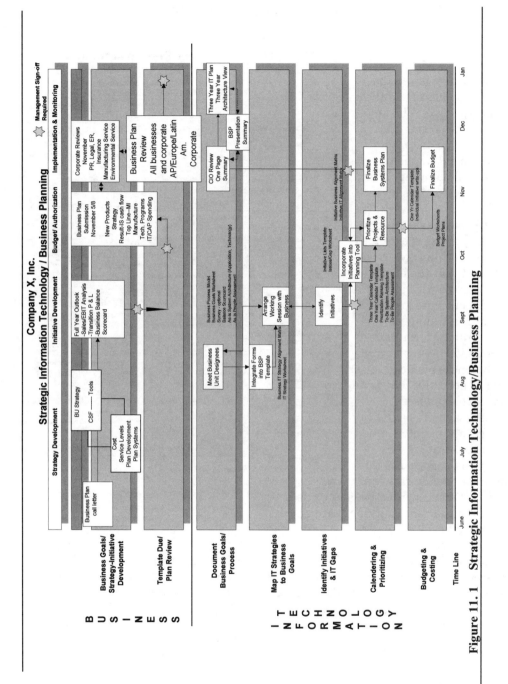

Figure 11.1 Strategic Information Technology/Business Planning

207

11. 1 Strategy Development – Business and Information Technology

Figure 11.1. 1   Strategy Development Phase

In Chapter 3 we reviewed the strategy development from the business perspective. The key ingredient to the strategy development stage is that it ensures alignment by the business and operational planning filtering across multiple business levels.

If the business strategy development process is extended to include the technology process, it is important that the business begins the process with an initial call to all the business groups. As mentioned in Chapter 3, enterprise strategy formulation begins with enterprise planning issuing a business plan call letter. This letter is normally sent to all the senior-level business executives for them to begin the process of gathering information relevant to the strategy formulation. In some cases this information is already gathered if the business is one that is proactive and focuses throughout the year on scenario planning and analysis.

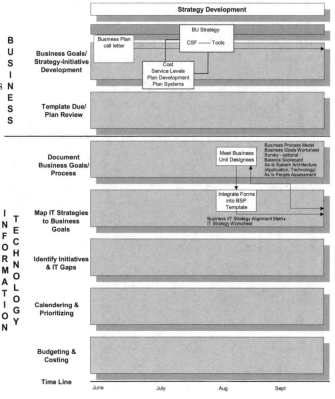

Plan development begins in earnest with the business trying to determine its strategic focus for the upcoming year. It does this by annotating its "critical success factors" that are important for the development of enterprise and business-level initiatives. In most cases, the business will try to determine the cost basis for the initiatives. They will then determine the appropriate services levels required to justify the amount of spending for the upcoming year against the initiatives.

In order to map the strategies, the IT function will need to focus on the following: a) the business goals and processes, b) the mapping of the information technology strategies to appropriate business goals, c) identify initiatives and potential IT Gaps, d) scheduling and prioritizing the technology initiative and e) budgeting and costing these initiatives. The specifics of each of the items listed above will be discussed later. The key to this phase is that the initiation of the plan should lag the beginning of the technology strategy process.

11. 2 Initiative Development – Business and Information Technology

The primary activity within the business function is to identify initiatives and prioritize them. These initiatives are prioritized against business drivers with integration of key factors such as cost, benefit, risk assessment, and budgetary issues.

In order to do that, the business-level executives within the business groups and corporate functional areas must plan effectively. If we examine the diagram to the right, we see that the general development of these initiatives takes a detailed analysis at a full-year outlook.

This full-year outlook could be extended to a one year -to-three year window. The limitation on the window is due to the fact that most business planning is limited to a maximum of three years because of the ever-changing business climate. A clear understanding of an industry's business drivers helps in determining the planning horizon.

Figure 11.2. 1 Initiative Development Phase-Business and Information Technology

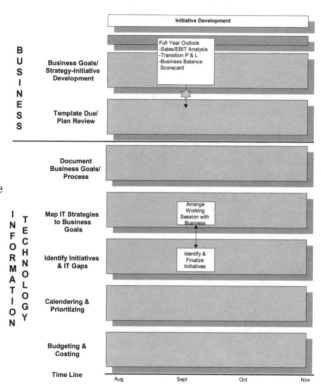

Within the IT environment, the focus will be to map the IT strategies to business goals. The end result of the full-year outlook or the three-year horizon will help determine the amount of business initiatives to be developed. At this point the technologist should learn what is important to the business and be able to track the upcoming IT strategies against the full-year business outlook to ensure consistency and alignment.

11. 3   Budgeting/Authorization – Business and Information Technology

The budget authorization process of the business should be consistent with what was outlined in Chapter 3. The process involves the collection of initiatives, the verification of the initiatives (through cost analysis and risk analysis), and benefit expectations.

Budget authorization usually occurs late in the year after all the initiatives within the business have been developed and fully cost justified. Cost justification is developed in the business plan submission that normally occurs in the November-to-December time frame prior to the upcoming year.

This by no means is an absolute, but it is important to have some formal process in place in order to institute complementing planning processes. The business plan submission would normally involve the stated full line of initiatives, potential cash flow impact, new product strategies and potential IT costs.

Figure 11.3. 1 Budgeting /Authorization Phase-Business and Information Technology

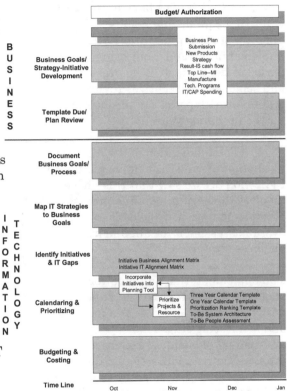

The focus on the technology side would be on the calendaring and prioritization of potential initiatives. A key note is that the final budget for IT initiatives is not derived within the budget authorization phase, but is usually lagged by a few months. It is important at the business level that the initiatives are outlined and agreed to by senior-level business executives while potential IT initiatives are defined later.

In most situations, funding for IT initiatives is usually not clearly defined during the overall planning phase, but is given just as a baseline. The detailed budget for IT initiatives is known after the *System Development Life Cycle* process begins.

11. 4 Implementation and Monitoring – Business and Information Technology

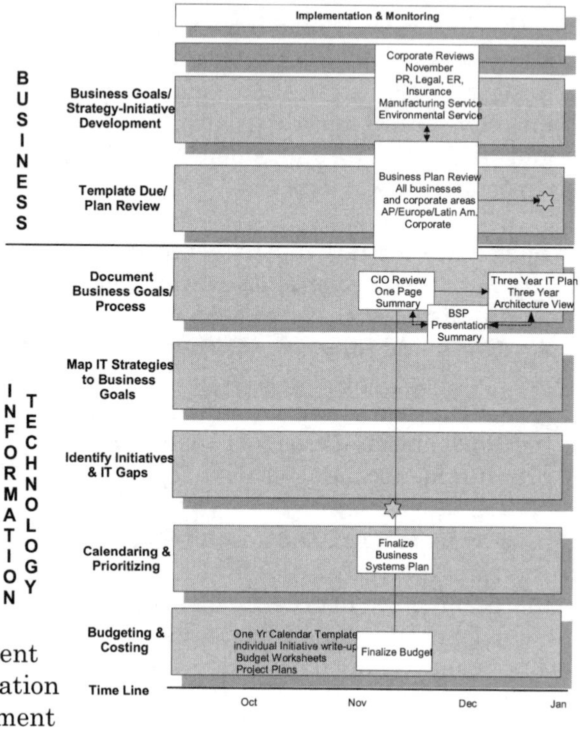

The implementation and monitoring phases of the overall planning cycle could be somewhat misleading. We normally think of implementation as the time when most initiatives have begun and will soon be producing results. The diagram at right illustrates how implementation and monitoring is a period of time when CEOs, presidents, and senior-level executives review and finalize all potential initiatives for the upcoming year.

Figure 11.4. 1 Implementation and Monitoring Phase - Business and Information Technology

The finalization of the initiatives is what is referred to as implementation. In Section 3.4 we saw that this phase involves the beginning of the process of implementation. This leads to the overall assessment for alignment with business strategy.

The implementation and monitoring stages for the IT function must be consistent with that of the business. The implementation and monitoring stages indicate the agreement and sign-off of business executives with the intended path and direction of the technology function. This is signaled by the completion and review of the business systems plan between the senior leader of the IT department (CIO) and the senior leader of the overall business (CEO). The agreement between the CIO and the CEO ensures three things:

1) the direction of the IT function; 2) money to be spent and the cost to maintain current systems; and 3) clear indication of IT's overall long- and short-term plans.

It is during this phase that the technology function can come to some clear understanding as to the availability of budgets and funds to support the technology direction.

12 *Information Technology View*

Up until now we have been focusing on the overlap between the planning activities of IT and the business. The main reason for this is to ensure alignment among the various functions. We will now start focusing on the information technology view. The IT view, as seen on page 215, focuses on the process activities that must be accomplished to ensure a complete, concise technology strategy.

An IT strategist must understand the fundamental processes that should be implemented to ensure alignment between technology and business direction. The IT view focuses on the beginning of the processes: from the time a user requests a system or application to the end of the actual planning cycle in preparation for the development of that system or application.

As the process is explained, view yourself as an IT strategist—someone who has been tasked to develop the appropriate strategy for the business. Imagine yourself as an IT strategist who will bring technology solutions to your company's business partners. The process involves the standard strategy development phases: 1) strategy development, 2) initiative development, 3) budget/authorization, and 4)implementation and monitoring.

On the vertical axis of the overall IT view are steps and tasks that must be completed in a systematic way to ensure success of the plan development. These include:

- Document Business Goals/Process: Various business processes are reviewed and the goals of the business are documented.
- Map IT Strategies to Business Goals: In this task the business goals are mapped against the developed and anticipated IT strategies.
- Identify Initiatives and Gaps: Initiatives are developed based on the goals and business processes. Commensurate with the development of the initiatives, the IT function must identify gaps that could hinder the initiative. Mitigators will be developed to address the gap actions.
- Calendaring and Prioritizing: This involves the documenting of potential IT initiatives on a one-year time horizon or a three-year time horizon. Documenting includes the priority and order in which these initiatives will be developed.
- Budgeting and Costing: Identify the amount of funds needed for the successful execution of a project.

Note that Sections 5.1 and 5.2 cover the content of the business systems plan. By the end of this process review, as an IT strategist, you will be able to cross-check the process with the development of the business systems plan. We will now examine the steps involved in the technology strategy process.

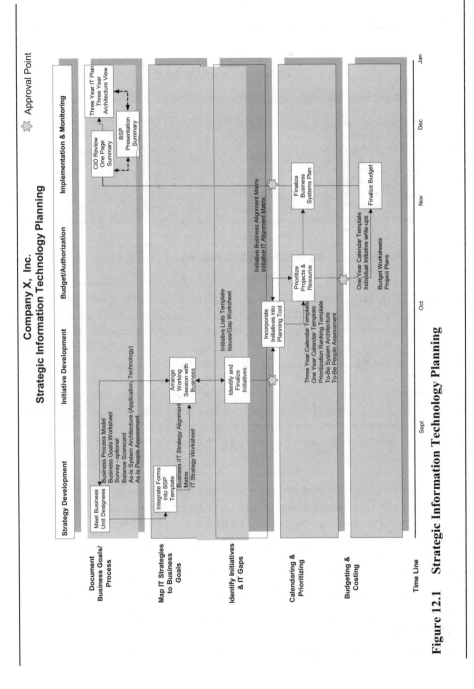

Figure 12.1 Strategic Information Technology Planning

12. 1   Strategy Development – Business Goal Process

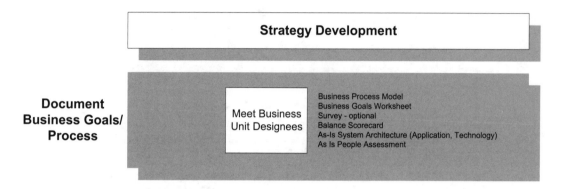

Figure 12.1. 1   Strategy Development – Business Goal Process

Description: Most IT failures are due to the misalignment of the technology strategy with the business strategy. Studies indicate that this is caused by the IT strategists not having adequate knowledge of the business. Before any technology solutions can be discussed, it is important for strategists to meet with their associates on the business side. These are their partners, but ultimately their customers.

Assuming this is a formal planning process, the business plan call has already been issued by the business. Once the business call has been issued, an event which normally occurs in the middle of the year, the strategist arranges a series of meetings with his business partners to understand what is on the table in terms of initiatives for the upcoming year.

These meetings should include not only the business partners, but senior-level officers from the business side who will be affected by the implemented technology. The initial meeting consists of a "meeting of the minds"—a time when the business partners can share their vision.

These meetings, as a whole, should serve the following outcomes:

- Clear and concise understanding of how the business operates;
- Understanding of the goals, missions, objectives and direction of the business;
- Understanding of the issues and challenges facing the business;

- Understanding of the strengths, weaknesses, opportunities and threats that the business encounters on a daily basis;

- Understanding of any internal or external regulatory activities affecting the business;

- Understanding of any compliance-related issues hindering the business from achieving its goals;

- Linkages between business objectives and strategies and those of the IT function.

The role of the IT strategist during these informal meetings is to listen and gain a full understanding about the needs of the business partners. Too often IT strategists offer their solutions without actually knowing and understanding the true needs of the business.

From these meetings, the IT strategist should be able to document in clear detail the business goals and processes of the business for the future years. The IT strategist also should focus on current technology architecture and determine the implications of the business processes being proposed.

Summary

Purpose:	To clearly document and understand the direction of the business. To understand the mission, goals, objectives, and strategies of the business.
Owner:	IT Strategist with input from the business owner
Input:	Business Goals Worksheets As-Is architecture As-Is People Assessment Business Process Model Data and Information Requirements
Process:	• Meet with business unit leaders • Document goals and objectives of the business • Achieve a clear understanding of where business unit is headed
Deliverable:	Complete list of strategies for business unit
Tools / Framework:	Strategic meetings with head of business group and/or corporate functional areas.
Cross Reference	Chapter 7 Strategies and Objectives

12. 2 Strategy Development – Map IT Strategies to Business Goals

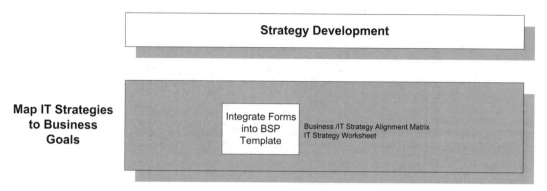

Figure 12.2. 1   Strategy Development – Map IT Strategies to Business Goals

Description: The first round of meetings between the IT strategist and the business partners gives initial direction as to where the IT strategist should be headed. At this time, he or she should remove themselves from their day-to-day IT activities and set apart time for analysis. This is still the strategy development phase and the IT strategist will perform analytical scenarios to arrive at possible technology strategies for the business.

This analytical time period could last anywhere from a couple of weeks to a whole month. What is most important is that the strategist determines an alignment link, which is the linkage of the business objective to the IT strategy to the IT initiative. This should not be an independent process by the technologist or the business partner. It should be a carefully orchestrated meeting with the business partner and the strategist.   The goal is to drive the business to take ownership of the potential IT initiatives and the alignment of these initiatives to business strategy.

This can be one of the most gut-wrenching sessions for the business partners. For each business objective, the strategist drives the senior business leader to declare how important the objective is to the completion of the technology strategy. Importance is based on a "1-to-3" scale rating with "1" being "not important" and "3" being "extremely important."   A complete description of how this procedure is executed is in Chapter 8.

The strategist begins the initial documentation of the *Business Systems Plan* based on the input from the business owner as it relates to the business direction and the completed alignment matrices.

Summary

Purpose:	To map the developed IT strategy to the business goals.
Owner:	IT Strategist with input from business owner
Input:	Strategic Business Technology Alignment Strategic Information Technology Alignment Strategic Business Alignment
Process:	• Take information gathered from initial business meetings. • Analyze impact of business initiatives on technology architecture. • Determine IT Strategies to be launched to support the business in the future. • Determine initial list of IT initiatives.
Deliverable:	Business/IT Strategy Alignment Matrix Preliminary List of Business Initiatives Preliminary List of IT initiatives
Tools / Framework:	• Strategic meetings with head of business group • Analytical brainstorm to determine IT strategy
Cross Reference	Chapter 7 Strategies and Objectives Chapter 8 Planning the Initiatives

12. 3 Initiative Development – Map IT Strategies to Business Goals

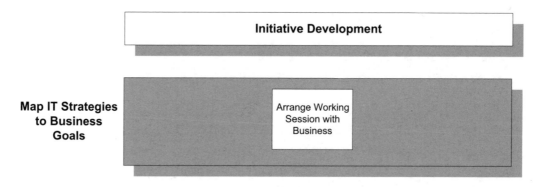

Figure 12.3. 1   Strategy Development – Map IT Strategies to Business Goals

Description: We have now moved from *Strategy Development* to *Initiative Development.* There is little or no separation in actual work activities between Strategy Development and Initiative Development as they relate to the mapping of strategies to business goals. The important activity from a process standpoint is that there will be continued working sessions between the IT strategist and their business partners. The continued meetings and working sessions will refine the list of initial initiatives and the continued changes to the alignment matrix.

At this time, the business and its overall strategic picture will be taking a look at its full-year outlook. The business should be evaluating the potential returns from the business initiatives. It also should be incorporating the preliminary cost of the IT initiatives on the overall cost structure. Additionally there should be an evaluation, from the business perspective, of the potential profit and loss impact of working on all the initiatives, both business and technology, or bypassing some for the following year. As the business performs this scenario analysis, the strategist also will be performing a scenario analysis as it relates to the initiatives and the impact they will have on the technology architecture and infrastructure.

Once the business has performed its various scenarios they relate to its business climate and the strategist has performed scenarios as they relate to the potential initiatives, working sessions are again arranged to address the potential and possible shift in direction of both the business and the technology environment. The hope is that these meetings will lead to a finalization of the initiatives list and also an agreement on the general direction of the IT function within the organization.

Summary

Purpose:	To further enhance the list of initiatives.
Owner:	IT strategist with input from business owner.
Input:	Strategic Business Technology Alignment Strategic Information Technology Alignment Strategic Business Alignment Initial List of Initiatives
Process:	▪ Gather the list of initial initiatives. ▪ Revisit the architectural map. ▪ Decipher the potential risk that exists with a possible technology solution. ▪ Revisit the alignment grid with the business owners to ensure agreement and consensus.
Deliverable:	Preliminary list of initiatives.
Tools / Framework:	▪ Strategic meetings with head of business group ▪ Analytical brainstorm to determine IT strategy ▪ Analytical meeting with technology development to determine impact
Cross Reference	Chapter 7 Strategies and Objectives Chapter 8 Planning the Initiatives

12. 4   *Initiative Development –Identify Initiatives and IT Gaps*

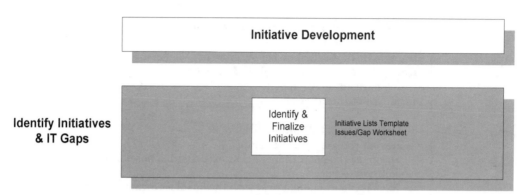

Figure 12.4. 1   Initiative Development – Identify Initiatives and IT Gaps

Description: Once the strategist and the business partners have agreed to the general direction of the business and the alignment matrix, in terms of the prioritization of IT initiatives, then the list can be finalized. In an iterative form, the IT strategist takes the list of major initiatives and consults with potential vendors to seek their input in the possibility of working on creating these initiatives. The finalized list is used as the final blueprint stamp of approval from the business to perform all the architectural and cost analysis to arrive at a final recommendation.

The strategist begins to develop a preliminary gap analysis worksheet as to the difference in the present state architecture versus what is needed to implement the new initiatives.

Summary

Purpose:	To finalize the list of initiatives for the upcoming year and 3-5 year planning horizon.
Owner:	Business Owner with help from IT Strategist
Input:	Business Process Model Strategic Business Technology Alignment Strategic Information Technology Alignment Strategic Business Alignment Final list of Initiatives
Process:	▪ Arrange working session with business owners. ▪ Agree on the alignment matrix ▪ Utilize alignment matrix to drive prioritization of initiatives ▪ Perform preliminary technology investigation for feasibility ▪ Finalize list of initiatives
Deliverable:	Final list of initiatives
Tools / Framework:	Strategic meetings with head of the business group Analytical brainstorm to determine technology feasibility
Cross Reference	Chapter 7 Strategies and Objectives Chapter 8 Planning the Initiatives

12. 5 Budget Authorization – Identify Initiatives and IT Gaps

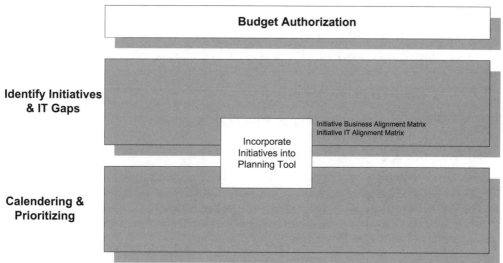

Figure 12.5. 1   Budget Authorization – Identify Initiatives and IT Gaps

Description: The IT strategist has received his/her preliminary walking papers to finalize the details on the potential initiatives. It should be understood between the strategist and the business partner that the finalization of the initiatives does not mean that the initiatives have cleared all hurdles and will be implemented. What it means is that the strategist can now investigate the feasibility of development and implementation of potential IT initiatives.

Now the most important activity for the strategist is to enter as many of the details known about the project into a project planning tool. This way the IT strategist can determine what kind of impact the initiatives will have on the relative resources of his group.

Too often projects are given the go-ahead without taking a look at the IT landscape in terms of resources and determining if new resources will be needed to develop the project. Resources are either dollars or personnel.

In some cases, depending on the size of the organization, the strategist will perform such an analysis or delegate it to a junior-level associate. This step, however, must be done before proceeding onto the prioritization of projects on the IT agenda.

As indicated on the previous diagram, incorporating the initiative into the planning tool occurs in two quadrants: *Identify Initiatives and IT* Gaps and *Calendaring and Prioritizing.* The step of incorporating the initiative into the planning tool can have an effect on the overall initiative identification. If it is determined that the resource is insufficient, the strategist might have to return to the business partner for more working sessions on determining how that issue can be mitigated. The lack of resource could effect the calendaring because it could be determined by the business partner that even though an initiative needs to be done, it will have to be done at a later date.

Summary

Purpose:	Take finalized list of initiatives and begin process of entering them into the planning tool.
Owner:	Business Owner with help from IT Strategist
Input:	Strategic Business Technology Alignment. Strategic Information Technology Alignment. Strategic Business Alignment. Final List of Initiatives.
Process:	▪ Begin preliminary data-gathering for each initiative; ▪ Receive input from potential vendor as to the structure of the initiative; ▪ Perform impact analysis on the organization impact of the new initiatives.
Deliverable:	Final list of initiatives.
Tools / Framework:	Analytical meeting with technology development to determine impact.
Cross Reference	Chapter 7 Strategies and Objectives Chapter 8 Planning the Initiatives Chapter 9 Key Tactical Initiative Chapter 10 The IT Organization and Strategies

12. 6 *Budget Authorization - Calendaring and Prioritizing*

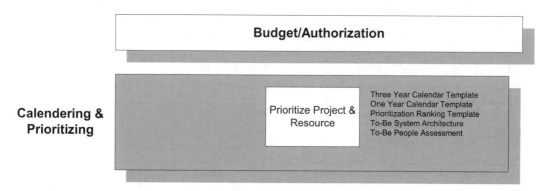

Figure 12.6. 1   Budget Authorization – Calendaring and Prioritizing

Description: This step strictly belongs to the IT strategist. At this point the strategist should have enough information to proceed with a complete analysis of the IT architecture and the initiative's impact on the organization or corporation. The key item for the strategist is to finalize the alignment matrix. The alignment matrix will determine the actual prioritization level of all the projects on the docket. This should be completed with the help of the business partner.

From the alignment matrix, with no conclusion on the relative strength of the technology organization, the strategist should place all the projects on a long-term calendar, three years out.

Once all the projects are laid out on a three-year scale, the IT strategist should perform an assessment on the overall technology function. The assessment should include: 1) the operational goals of the people, processes, and technology within the function, 2) an evaluation of all the common technologies, 3) a view of the possible company-wide technology efforts that are on-going or have a potential to be developed from the current initiatives, 4) investigate the possibility of shared technology solutions in terms of out-sourcing, infrastructure and emerging technologies, and 5) a comprehensive look at the non-standard and first-time use technology in the function.

This assessment will help develop a potential boundary in which the IT function can operate—given the number of IT initiatives in the pipeline. The strategist can then determine the one-year picture. The one-year picture will be driven by time and by resources. If the number of initiatives increases, time and/or resources will have to be added. Time and resources will offset each other as they relate to the relative success of a project.

The key point for the strategist is to develop from the list of initiatives the potential impact these initiative will have on the architecture. This will help the strategist drive to *a to-be Architecture* (see Section 5.3). This is not a simple effort. It requires knowledge of data, processes, and technologies that exist within the company and are available on the open market.

The development of the key initiative list; the as-is and to-be architecture; people assessment; the one-year calendar; and the three-year calendar are all key components to the completion and finalization of the overall strategy.

Summary

Purpose:	To finalize the priority of projects for the upcoming year or planning landscape.
Owner:	IT Strategist
Input:	Three-Year Calendar Template One-Year Calendar Template Prioritization Ranking Template To-Be System Architecture To-Be People Assessment Final list of Initiatives
Process:	▪ Perform more detail data gathering for each initiative; ▪ Determine impact of initiative on architecture; ▪ Determine the three year calendar; ▪ Perform assessment of people in IT Department; ▪ Determine one-year calendar.
Deliverable:	Final list of initiatives with time restraints
Tools / Framework:	Analytical session with IT strategist and IT department heads
Cross Reference	Chapter 8 Planning the Initiatives Chapter 9 Key Tactical Initiative Chapter 10 The IT Organization and Strategies

12. 7 Implementation and Monitoring – Calendaring and Prioritizing

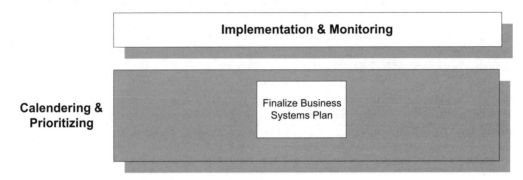

Figure 12.7. 1   Implementation & Monitoring – Calendaring and Prioritizing

Description: The strategist, with help from leads in the IT department, can now develop a comprehensive business systems plan. The business systems plan is an agreement document drafted between the strategist and the business partner. It serves as a "bible" between the business and the IT department as to the direction of the business and technology.

Summary

Purpose:	Create a *Business Systems Plan* from information and data collected during strategy development, initiative development, and budget authorization processes.
Owner:	IT Strategist
Input:	Business Process Model Strategic Business Technology Alignment Strategic Information Technology Alignment Strategic Business Alignment Three-Year Calendar Template One-Year Calendar Template Prioritization Ranking Template To-Be System Architecture To-Be People Assessment Key Initiative List & Categorization Final list of Initiatives

Process:	<ul><li>Gather all information;</li><li>Follow steps from Section 5 to create Business Systems Plan.</li></ul>
Deliverable:	Business Systems Plan
Tools / Framework:	Analytical session with IT Strategist and IT Department Heads.
Cross Reference	Chapter 7 Strategies and Objectives Chapter 8 Planning the Initiatives Chapter 9 Key Tactical Initiative Chapter 10 The IT Organization and Strategies

12. 8 Implementation and Monitoring – Budgeting and Costing

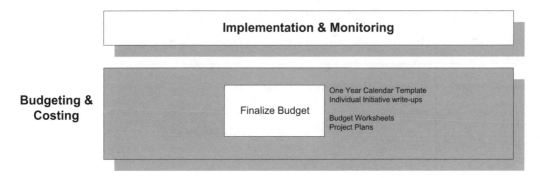

Figure 12.8. 1   Implementation & Monitoring – Budgeting and Costing

Description: The strategist will utilize, if available, his junior analyst to determine the potential cost for a particular initiative. The creation of the finalized budget includes as much detail information that can be gathered about a particular initiative. The strategist should know all the detail of the key initiative as outlined in Section 5.2.4.

Once information is finalized on each project, the strategist will utilize the *Key Initiative List and Categorization* (Section 5.2.4) to detail all initiatives for the upcoming year. The summary of all initiatives' cost will help to finalize the budget.

Budget finalization, however, does not occur until the key initiatives are summarized along with the maintenance and other material. The technology budget should include money for new initiatives, but it also should include money for maintenance (Section 5.2.1.).

Summary

Purpose:	Arrive at a completed budget based on the number of technology initiatives to be undertaken.
Owner:	IT Strategist with assistance from the business partner.
Input:	Final List of Initiatives. Key Initiative List and Categorization.

Process:	▪ Gather all information from vendor; ▪ Cumulate and summarize the cost findings of all initiatives.
Deliverable:	Business Systems Plan.
Tools / Framework:	Analytical session with IT strategist and IT department heads.
Cross Reference	Chapter 6 Executive Summary Chapter 8 Key Tactical Initiative

12. 9 Implementation and Monitoring – Goals and Process

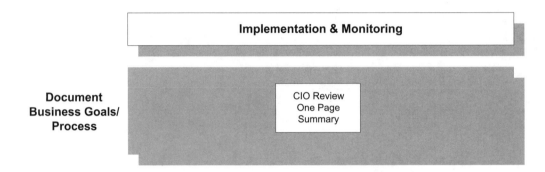

Figure 12.9. 1   Implementation and Monitoring – Goals and Process

Description: One of the many duties of IT strategists is to think through complicated problems and arrive at viable solutions. They need to simplify all the information gathered from tactical, strategic and brainstorming meetings and condense it into a one-page summary for the CIO.

Let's assume that the CIO has many different business units and corporate functional areas that he/she is overseeing. The CIO would need a simple one-page summary detailing the activities of each business unit or each corporate functional area. Here's an example of such a one-page summary:

Table 12.9. 1   Summary Example

Aircraft Systems Division

Focus on :
- Improve sales effectiveness and efficiency
- Increase forecast accuracy
- Make ASD more customer friendly
- Enable productivity improvements
- Streamline supply chain activities
- Improve financial and analysis tools
- Identify revenue opportunities using analytical tools

2001 Planned Budget ($M) – $8,621.4
- Infrastructure
  - Salaries $1,800
  - Depreciation/Maint $2,600
  - Consulting $1,650
  - Other $0

- Projects
  - Expense $750
  - Depreciation $50

- Corporate IT Allocation $1,771.4

2000 budget ($M) - $8,618.4 (Corporate IT Alloc $M 1,648.4)

2001 Capital Plan $650

Top Strategic Projects – Business Focus

Strategic Initiatives	Improved Operating Margins	Growth International to 50%	Sales Volume Growth	Improve Earnings Per Share	Customer Needs	Operational Excellence	Infra-structure	Job Order Date/Total Cost($k)	Estimated Costs ($k) to BU in 2001	
									Capital	Expense
Baan Euro Upgrade		X		X	X		X	Q301/$300	100	200
Sales Reporting Improvements	X		X	X	X	X		Q201/$50	0	100
Intranet Improvements	X			X		X	X	Q301/$50	0	50
LIMS-Baan Interface	X			X		X		Q401/$100	0	100
Sales/Intranet/Lims Servers							X	Q101/$250	250	0
Baan and JBA Enhancements	X			X	X	X	X	Q301/$50	0	200
Shop Floor/AS400 Capacity						X	X	Q301/$400	300	100

Summary

Purpose:	Arrive at a completed budget based on the number of IT initiatives to be undertaken.
Owner:	IT Strategist
Input:	Key Initiative List and Categorization Final list of Initiatives Strategic theme
Process:	· Take all key initiatives from the Business Systems Plan. · Cross-check initiatives with the strategic theme to ensure that the key initiative addresses one or many strategic themes outlined by the CEO. · Summarize the information onto one page.
Deliverable:	One-Page Business Summary
Tools / Framework:	Analytical session with IT strategist and business partner.
Cross Reference	Chapter 6 Executive Summary Chapter 8 Key Tactical Initiative

12. 10   Implementation and Monitoring – Goals and Process – View and Summary

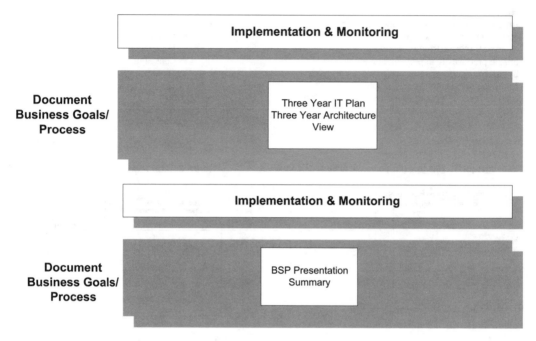

Figure 12.10. 1   Implementation and Monitoring – Goals and Process – View and Summary

Description: Why are there two functional steps on this page? The three-year *IT Plan* and the three-year *IT Architecture View* are parts of the business systems plan that will be pulled and used in any presentation that has to be made to senior executives or business partners.   The BSP presentation summary is a culmination at the enterprise level of all the one-page documents from all businesses and corporate functional areas.

The presentation summary is used by the CIO to the CEO and summarizes the list of activities across the organization's IT landscape.   This summary is a detailed document that includes not only the one-page summaries, but also a roll-up of investment activities for all businesses.

The document shows the overall technology investment for all the enterprise businesses. It serves as a detailed library for the CIO to detail to the CEO the alignment or non-alignment of the IT function with the rest of the enterprise.

Here is an example:

Summary

Purpose:	Develop a comprehensive document that represents the outlook and direction of the IT function.
Owner:	IT Strategist or other senior-level IT personnel.
Input:	All Business Systems Plans from all business and corporate functional areas
Process:	• Gather all one-page summaries from all businesses and corporate functional areas. • Develop a Summary Presentation in the format above.
Deliverable:	Business Systems Plan Summary
Tools / Framework:	Business Systems Plan One-Page Summary
Cross Reference	

13   *Scenario Analysis and Planning – Impact on IT Futures*

Scenario Analysis vs. Standard Planning

Ideally, the planning process is a once-a-year activity that should be monitored and revisited throughout the year. Sometimes the question is asked: "Given today's economy, is once-a-year planning enough?" The answer is no.

Some feel the alternative is to decide whether to do strategic planning or scenario analysis. Personally, I highly recommend and regard the concept of *Intermittent Scenario Planning* (ISP) to complement the normal strategic planning cycle.

Scenario Analysis

What if the business environment changes? What if the Internet disrupts the base foundation on which the business is based? What if new technology arises that creates strategic uncertainty? Any drastic or fundamental change in the way the organization operates—strategy, vision, objective, goals—will necessitate a change.

A plan is a plan and as such it can change. The next question, however, is: "What direction should we change?" Are there alternative futures available that do not require an immediate decision, but require an immediate awareness? According to Eric Clemons, who is a professor at the Wharton School of Business and writer of the article "Using Scenario Analysis to Manage the Strategic Risks of Reengineering," "Firms either attempt too little, creating functionality risk, or attempt whatever change is necessary, creating political risk."

This is true of scenario analysis workshops. My suggestion is that leaders within the IT department and strategic thinkers in the business community remove themselves from the business environment. I recommend a retreat-type location where they can focus on entertaining possible risks that could endanger their survival.

Scenario Analysis should complement the *IT Strategic Planning* process. Developing the business plan, finalizing a budget and implementing systems are all part of the process. However, on a time line, scenario planning should also be occurring sometime during the year.

It is important for both business and technology professionals to assess the risks associated with any and all initiative development and deployment. The probability of increased risks will affect the results of the initiative. There are risks associated with the general business and the IT environment as well as risks associated with a particular project implementation.

General Environment Risk

There are two kinds of general risk specific to any business or IT environment: *functional risk* and *political risk*.

Functional risk is managing wrong changes to systems and processes. Whenever a firm decides to undergo IT re-engineering, there is always the possibility that the changes the senior executives and change management experts believe are necessary, are not. In such cases mitigation is needed to address the possibility that the proposed changes might result in business disruption, discontinuity, or failure.

Political risk relates to potential changes to systems and processes that will yield a negative response or acceptance from influencers within the organization. Some projects can be successful and receive less than concrete acceptance due to the acceptance level of the key influencers.

It is necessary that all projects have complete and clear management of potential functional risk and political risk before moving on to implementation.

General Large Implementation Risk

There are five risks associated with any large project implementation: 1) *financial risk*, 2) *technical risk*, 3) *project risk*, 4) *functionality risk*, and 5) *political risk*.

All successful projects are managed with three things in mind. This is called "the triad of success": all successful projects were managed 1) on schedule, 2) on budget, and 3) met the satisfaction of the customer. Understanding the triad of success is a key component in understanding and applying the risk associated with any implementation.

Financial risk is associated with cost overrun and scope changes during the normal process of technology development and implementation. For example, a change mandated by the business can leave the IT department no alternative but to go along with the change without the proper understanding that the mandated change will result in a cost overrun.

Technical risk means that the time allotted for implementation is too long a period and will render the new technology obsolete. In our fast- moving society it is not uncommon for today's cutting-edge technology to be tomorrow's antiquated system. Both business and technology personnel need to be aware of the IT environment and implement strategies that address the rapid acceleration in technology development.

Project risk is associated with the failure of a project. This risk is inherent in all projects, but is mitigated by savvy project managers who have focused on the triad of success—schedule, budget, and satisfaction.

Functionality risk is similar to project risk, but the difference is that this risk takes into consideration what was promised versus what is delivered. Functionality risk and project risk complement each other in that functionality risk drives project risk. If a project does not deliver what is promised, the likelihood is that it will be viewed as a failure.

Political risk is the risk associated with an organization's resistance to a particular business process change or a technology implementation. In an organization, the leaders might drive a business process change, but it is the actual users who use the new system. A failure of the users to buy into the particular change will lead to increased political risk, which could create project failure.

Scenario Analysis and Planning

There are three fundamental parts to the *Scenario Analysis and Planning* Process: 1) re-visioning, 2) futures, and 3) strategy development. In re-visioning, the focus is to revise the fundamental business mission and competitive strategy to reflect any future state.

Re-Visioning

Re-visioning is a process that involves both business and technology leaders assessing whether the mission of their organization is the same as it was in the prior period. Prior period could mean weeks, months, or years, depending on the type of industry. In re-visioning, an organization's leaders and subordinates review the entire landscape of the business. This involves a review of all work processes, work flows, job descriptions, and IT systems.

The important concept of re-visioning is to accept the fact that nothing is spared when taking a fundamental review of an organization's mission. The revision, while taking peripheral views of competitors and their strategies, will help drive the future state.

For example, looking at a particular work process determines there is a need to get information in the hands of sales agent in the fields. The fact that the work process needs to change is not the most important item, it is the time that the process needs to be changed. If the competitor is not aware of the need to change, then by default, the first to the table in terms of determining the need for work process change will have a first-mover advantage.

Futures

The documentation and elaboration of the alternative futures that exist is paramount to the success of scenario analysis and planning.

In this part of scenario planning, the business and IT professionals will determine the range of futures that might exist given the result of the re-visioning effort.

Determining the futures is a relatively easy process. What is difficult is the willingness of those involved to be open to the many potential futures that might exist in a business. Who knew that the personal computer would have such a dynamic effect on people? Who knew what the impact of the Internet would have on society?

Some of us were there during the implementation of all these futures—we either learned about it or caught on right away. Those who caught on quickly enough are now millionaires, even billionaires. Someone had to embrace the alternative future. The most important part of the scenario process is not to leave an alternative future as something that is impossible, but to try and plan for the impossible.

Strategy Development

Once we complete the re-visioning process and have accepted the various futures that exist, it is then time to develop strategies that addresses the potential futures. Strategy development involves acknowledging that there are uncertainties and then developing a range of strategies to address future scenarios.

When

When does the scenario analysis and planning session occur? Bi-monthly? Quarterly? Planning should be executed at a particular time. There is a time for formal planning, which is fundamental in stabilizing any organization. After stabilization, there needs to be random scenario analysis and planning. It does not matter when, where, or why. The important thing is that scenario planning should be an "ever-greening" process—a repetitive process that occurs numerous times during the year. The frequency of scenario planning and analysis is left up to the organization and it depends on the industry.

What Scenario Analysis is Not

I recently heard it stated that scenario analysis will lead to a complete conclusion as to the future state of an industry. I disagree. Scenario planning and analysis neither leads to a singular strategy nor a single answer to the future. It leads to many different possibilities.

Organizations employ senior-level executives to devise the right answer for what the future holds, as each organization experience both success and failure, and high's and lows in the industry in their lifetime. These same executives are also the main obstacle in determining the future. Why? These executives oftentimes have a myopic view of the future that limits the potential of the organization.

Scenario analysis and planning does not hide uncertainty and ambiguity. It embraces it. It enjoys it and it looks to uncertainty and ambiguity as opportunities for the future.

14 *Appendix*

14.1 Bibliography

BOAR, B. *The Art of Strategic Planning for Information Technology.*
New York: John Wiley & Sons, Inc., 1993.

CLEMONS, E. K. "Using Scenario Analysis to Manage the Strategic Risks of
Reengineering." *Sloan Management Review,* Summer 1995:61-71

HAX, A. C. and N. S. MAJLUF. *The Strategy Concept and Process*.
New Jersey: Prentice Hall, 1996.

LABROVITZ, G. and ROSANSKY, *The Power of Alignment.*
New York: John Wiley & Sons, Inc. 1997.

MINTZBERG, H. and J. B. Quinn, *The Strategy Process – Concepts, Contexts, Cases.*
New Jersey: Prentice Hall, 1996.

SPEWAK, S. H. *Enterprise Architecture Planning.*
New York: John Wiley & Sons, Inc. 1992.

14.2 Notes

Chapter 1: Understanding Information Technology

1. Conversation with W. Taranda from Arc Partners utilized in the refining of the High Level View of IT, January 2000.

Chapter 2: Understanding The Business Before IT

1. Conversation and discussion with B. Gray and UMT consultants utilized in the refining of the Organizational Planning Process, October 1997.

Chapter 3 – The Phases of the Business Process

1. Conversation and discussion with B. Gray and UMT consultants utilized in the refining of the Strategy Development Phase, October 1997.
2. Discussion with E. Nash and UMT consultants utilized in the refining of the Initiative Development and Planning Phases, October 1997.
3. Discussion with E. Nash and UMT consultants utilized in the refining of the Budget and Prioritization Phase, October 1997.
4. Conversation and discussion with B. Gray and UMT consultants utilized in the refining of the Implementation and Monitoring Phase, October 1997.

14.3 *Index*

14.4 *Table of Figures*

14.5 Table of Tables

14.6   Business Systems Plans Content

Business Systems Plans

The *Business Systems Plan* calls for the following five sections:

1. Executive Summary
    - Overview of the entire document
    - Strategic, other development, infrastructure, business as usual, year 2000, and chargeback costs
    - Resource and cost estimates

2. Strategies and Objectives
    - Business Unit's Mission, Goals, Objectives and Strategies
    - Key Information Technology Strategies
    - Strategic Alignment/ issues affecting systems strategy
    - Business Goals Worksheet (3 columns)
    - Business-IT Strategic Alignment

3. Initiative Planning
    - Expansion of Business Goals Worksheet
    - Strategic IT Alignment
    - Strategic Business Alignment
    - Pictorial View – Three-Year Plan
    - System Architecture Diagram
    - Critical Success Factors/Dependencies

4. Key Initiatives for the Coming Year
    - Initiative List and Categorization
    - Pictorial View – One-Year Plan
    - Detailed View of each Key Initiative
    - Strategic Themes

5. Business Unit IT Landscape and Strategies
    - Overall technology direction
    - Progress planned toward the target environment

6. Potential Key Initiatives
    - Major initiatives that did not make the "cut"
    - Alternative means to launch these initiatives

15 *Business Systems Planning Template*

DRAFT

Business Systems Plan

[Insert Year Here]

[Insert Business Group Name Here]

[Insert Company Name]

[Insert Date Here]

Table of Contents

Executive Summary

Business Systems Plan Overview

Summarize the plan and context in one paragraph.

Information Technology Budget Expectation and Categorization

Include your budget expectation for the upcoming year and categorize it as displayed below.

	20xx Budget ($000)		
	Discretionary	Non-Discretionary	Total
Strategic Development	0		0
Tactical Development	0		0
Infrastructure Development	0		0
Salaries		0	0
Depreciation, Maintenance		0	0
Business As Usual		0	0
Year 20xx Industry Initiatives		0	0
Corporate IT Allocation		0	0
Total	$0	$0	$0
20xx Capital Plan			$0

Key Initiatives List and Requirements

Highlight and characterize the nature of your initiatives by completing the following table. We would expect in the range of 6-12 initiatives for most groups.

The criteria for including Key Initiatives are as follows:

- Has a significant impact on meeting Business Unit's (BG) performance objectives.
- Requires resources to meet government mandated requirements.
- Are of a high visibility nature (internal or external) OR
- Fit one or more criteria of the risk profile:

  ◊ new technologies or development methodologies
  ◊ first use of a technology
  ◊ cross Business Unit initiative
  ◊ dependence on outside entities (vendors, consultants third parties) for the success of the project
  ◊ requires hardware or software R&D activities
  ◊ does not conform with established standards of guidelines
  ◊ needs infrastructure upgrades
  ◊ major shift from old infrastructure to new infrastructure (e.g. shift from heavy printing to image and on-line report retrieval)
  ◊ provides information access to external customers

Initiatives	Required Resources		$ Estimated / Allocated ($000)			Return on Investment Justification
	Full Time Employees	Consultants	Total Project	2002 Estimated	2002 Allocated	
Initiative 1	0	0	0	0	0	
Initiative 2	0	0	0	0	0	
Initiative 3	0	0	0	0	0	
Initiative 4	0	0	0	0	0	
Initiative 5	0	0	0	0	0	
Initiative 6	0	0	0	0	0	
Initiative 7	0	0	0	0	0	
Initiative 8	0	0	0	0	0	
Initiative 9	0	0	0	0	0	
Initiative 10	0	0	0	0	0	
Initiative 11	0	0	0	0	0	
Initiative 12	0	0	0	0	0	
Initiative 13	0	0	0	0	0	
Initiative 14	0	0	0	0	0	
Initiative 15	0	0	0	0	0	
Total	0	0	$0	$0	$0	

Compliance and External Regulatory Initiatives

Highlight all initiatives from the previous list that are compliance and/or external regulatory initiatives.

Other Important Items

Describe any important items that are not otherwise captured in the document (optional).

Strategies and Objectives

Business Unit's Mission

Insert Business Group's Mission. Please reference other planning documents as appropriate for these topics

Business Unit's Goals

Insert Business Group's Goals

Business Unit's Objectives

Insert Business Group's Objectives

Business Unit's Strategies/Processes

Insert Business Group's Strategies and state succinctly how these will be achieved.
Insert Business Process Model

Key Information Technology Strategies

Insert Business Group's IT Strategies and state succinctly any issues related Global IT objectives and direction.

Strategic Alignment Issues/Gaps

Highlight strategic issues such as, the need to retrain a large part of the IT staff, large upgrade to the infrastructure, a shift in the dollars expended to "keep the lights on"(BAU), significant change in business strategy affecting systems strategy, etc.

Business Unit Goals Outline

Complete the first three columns of the business goal worksheet,

Title: I.T. **STRATEGY WORKSHEET**
Organization: XYZ Corporation. **Business Unit:** **Date:** 7/23/97 Page 1 of 2

Business Processes / I.T. Alignment	BUSINESS OBJECTIVES	I.T. STRATEGY TO SUPPORT BUS. OBJECTIVES	I.T. INITIATIVES	PRIORITY (H, M, L)
DEVELOP & COMMERCIALIZE TECHNOLOGY				
CREATE MARKET				
MANAGE CUSTOMER RELATIONS				
PLAN PRODUCTION OPERATIONS				
MANAGE SUPPLY SOURCING				
PROCESS ORDERS				
PRODUCE PRODUCT				
MANAGE INVENTORY & DISTRIBUTION				

Strategic Business Technology Alignment

Please indicate the alignment of IT strategies to the business objectives listed in the introduction.

		Business Objectives								
IT Strategies	Objective 1	Objective 2	Objective 3	Objective 4	Objective 5	Objective 6	Objective 7	Objective 8	Objective 9	Objective 10
IT Strategies 1										
IT Strategies 2										
IT Strategies 3										
IT Strategies 4										
IT Strategies 5										
IT Strategies 6										
IT Strategies 7										
IT Strategies 8										
IT Strategies 9										
IT Strategies 10										
IT Strategies 11										
IT Strategies 12										
IT Strategies 13										
IT Strategies 14										
IT Strategies 15										

Business Objective Legend

1 ~ Low impact to business objective

2 ~ Medium impact to business objective

3 ~ High impact to business objective

Initiatives Planning

Strategic IT Alignment

Please indicate the alignment of initiatives to the IT Strategies listed in the introduction.

Initiatives	IT Strategy 1	IT Strategy 2	IT Strategy 3	IT Strategy 4	IT Strategy 5	IT Strategy 6	IT Strategy 7	IT Strategy 8	IT Strategy 9	IT Strategy 10
					Information Technology Strategies					
Initiative 1										
Initiative 2										
Initiative 3										
Initiative 4										
Initiative 5										
Initiative 6										
Initiative 7										
Initiative 8										
Initiative 9										
Initiative 10										
Initiative 11										
Initiative 12										
Initiative 13										
Initiative 14										
Initiative 15										

IT Strategies Legend

1 ~ Low impact to IT strategy   2 ~ Medium impact to IT strategy   3 ~ High impact to IT strategy

Strategic Business Alignment

Please indicate the alignment of initiatives to the business objectives listed in the introduction.

Business Systems Plan - Insert Business Unit Name Here

Initiatives	Objective 1	Objective 2	Objective 3	Objective 4	Objective 5	Objective 6	Objective 7	Objective 8	Objective 9	Objective 10
					Business Objectives					
Initiative 1										
Initiative 2										
Initiative 3										
Initiative 4										
Initiative 5										
Initiative 6										
Initiative 7										
Initiative 8										
Initiative 9										
Initiative 10										
Initiative 11										
Initiative 12										
Initiative 13										
Initiative 14										
Initiative 15										

Business Objective Legend

1 ~ Low impact to business objective   2 ~ Medium impact to business objective   3 ~ High impact to business objective

Pictorial View – Three Year Plan

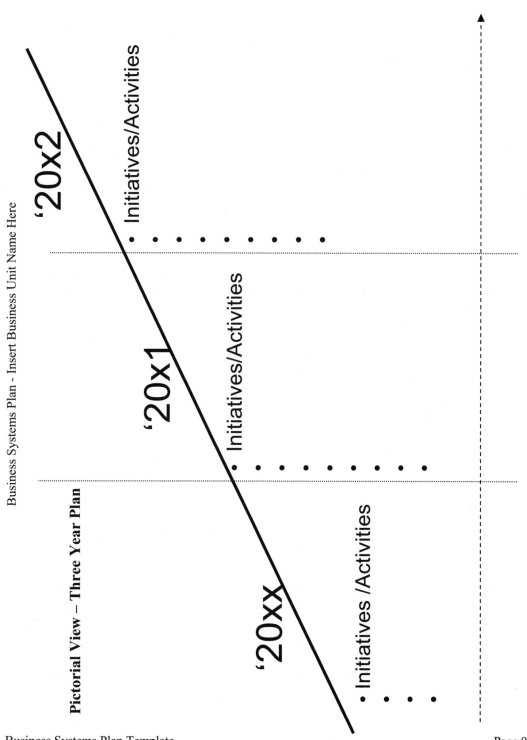

'20x2

'20x1

'20xx

- Initiatives/Activities
- Initiatives/Activities
- Initiatives /Activities

System Architecture Diagram

Please insert system architecture diagram reflecting current state and expected state within three years.

Critical Success Factors/Dependencies

Key Initiatives for the Coming Year

Key Initiatives List and Categorization

Initiatives	Business Justification: Increase Revenue	Decrease Cost	Increased Quality	Increased Compliance/Control	Enable Business Strategy	Operational Necessity	Increased Decision Support	Increased Customer Service	Important Technologies: Image	Workflow	Data Warehousing	Voice Response Units	Call Center Technology	Internet Technologies	MPP Large Scale Computing	Electronic Commerce	Wireless Communication	Computer Telephony	New Devl. Methodologies	Schedule Estimates: Best Case	Worst Case	2002 Avg FTE: Full Time Employees	Consultants	$ Est/Alloc ($000): Total Project	2001 Estimated	2001 Allocated
Initiative 1									X										X	2Q02	4Q02	0	0	0	0	0
Initiative 2											X										1Q02	0	0	0	0	0
Initiative 3											X	X	X							3Q02	3Q02	0	0	0	0	0
Initiative 4									X		X	X	X								3Q02	0	0	0	0	0
Initiative 5											X										1Q02	0	0	0	0	0
Initiative 6									X		X	X	X								3Q02	0	0	0	0	0
Initiative 7									X		X		X							3Q02	1Q02	0	0	0	0	0
Initiative 8											X										3Q02	0	0	0	0	0
Initiative 9									X		X	X	X							3Q02	1Q02	0	0	0	0	0
Initiative 10									X		X	X	X							3Q02	3Q02	0	0	0	0	0
Initiative 11											X										1Q02	0	0	0	0	0
Initiative 12									X		X	X	X							3Q02	3Q02	0	0	0	0	0
Initiative 13									X		X										3Q02	0	0	0	0	0
Initiative 14									X		X										1Q02	0	0	0	0	0
Initiative 15									X		X		X							3Q02	1Q02	0	0	0	0	0
Total																						0	0	$0	$0	$0

Business Justification Legend

1 ~ Low impact to business justification   2 ~ Medium impact to business justification   3 ~ High impact to business justification

Pictorial View – One-Year Plan
20XX Systems Strategic Plan - Major Initiatives

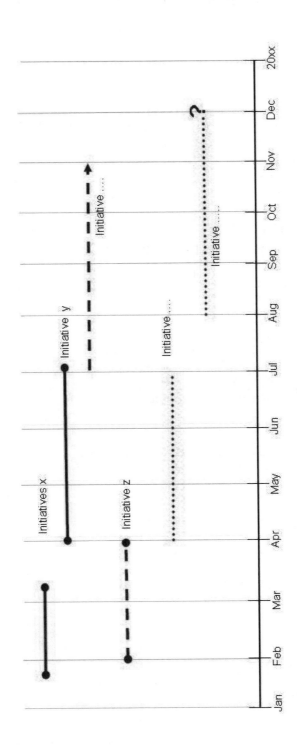

Insert Key Initiative Name

Description

Provide a brief description of the overall initiative, its overall objectives and timing.

Business Purpose

Identify the business purpose (e.g., process improvement, product stewardship, call center, financial accounting, etc.).

Initiative Result/Deliverables

Specifically state the system and/or components that will be built.

Initiative Approach

Provide a general overview of the approach to launch this initiative.

Activities		Time Estimates
I.	Examine and Prepare System Environment	X Weeks
	•	
II.	Installation and Configuration	X Weeks
	•	
III.	Application Conversion	X Weeks
	•	
IV.	Testing and Modification	X Weeks
	•	
V.	Implementation	X Weeks
	•	

Initiative Economics/Staffing and Budget

Insert the initiative economics in the table below and briefly state staffing and budgetary information.

	Estimated	Allocated
Current Year Cost	0	0
Current Year Revenue Contribution	0	0
Currrent Year Cost Savings	0	0
Net	$ -	$ -
Total Project Cost	0	0
Capital Expenditure		
Current Year Capital Expenditure	0	0
Total Project Captial Expenditure	0	0

Resource	Hrs/week	# of weeks	Company X	Consultant	External $	Total Cost
Project Lead (¼ time)			X			
Business Personnel (½ time)						
One FTE (TBD)			X	X		
½ IT Infrastructure Member			X			

Technology Requirements

Insert detailed list of technologies associated with the initiatives.

Sub-projects

Provide sub-project information (optional).

Changes to ongoing and non-discretionary activities

Provide information related to changes to ongoing and non-discretionary activities based on these initiatives.

Links to Enterprise-Wide Initiatives

Known enterprise initiatives
Proposed enterprise initiatives

Initiatives Risk Assessment

Questions	High	Medium	Low
What is the probability that scope will change over the initiative's duration?			X
What is the organizational impact of the initiative?	X		
What is the probability of success being measurable?			X
What is the regulatory impact upon the initiative?	X		
What is the emerging technology impact upon the initiative?	X		
What is the impact of outsourcing upon the initiative?			X
What is the impact of a vendor package upon the initiative?	X		
What is the likelihood of the business drivers changing over the initiative's duration?			X
To what extent does the initiative require operations and business participation?		X	

Strategic Themes

For each initiative, state clearly the relationship to each category.

Initiatives	Sales and Marketing			Touching the Customer			Information Advantage			Infrastructure								Technology Innovation			
	Contact Management	Information Analytics	Sales Tracking	Electronic Interaction	House-holding	Ware-housing	Quality	Delivery	Mining	Desktop Technology Upgrades	Major Increases in Processing Power Communications or DASD	Shift from One Processing Environment to Another	Image	Workflow	Data Warehousing	Voice Response Units	Call Center Technology	Internet/Intranet	MPP Large Scale Computing	Electronic Commerce	Wireless Communications
Initiative 1	X						X	X		X			X								
Initiative 2		X			X	X		X		X			X			X					
Initiative 3				X				X	X		X	X					X		X	X	X
Initiative 4									X											X	
Initiative 5			X	X		X	X	X			X		X		X		X		X		
Initiative 6	X	X		X			X				X		X				X				
Initiative 7							X			X				X							
Initiative 8			X							X		X									
Initiative 9		X					X						X								X
Initiative 10				X				X			X	X	X			X					X
Initiative 11	X				X			X	X	X						X					
Initiative 12	X				X	X				X			X				X				
Initiative 13		X		X				X			X	X									
Initiative 14																			X		
Initiative 15				X				X	X		X		X								

Business Unit IT Landscape & Strategies

Operational Goals

Paint the picture of where your organization is now and how much progress you expect to make during the year in terms of the following dimensions.

People

Insert information related to staff, skills, etc.

Processes

Insert information related to program/project initiation, application development methodologies, and other related processes.

Technology

Insert information related to new technologies, standards, and architecture.

Common Technologies

List common technologies or technical attributes of initiatives.

Enterprise-wide Technology Efforts

List linkages to enterprise-wide technology efforts, e. g., image, workflow.

Possible Shared Technology Solutions

List possible technology solutions that may be shared across the organization.

Outsourcing

Include details on outsourcing and other external sourcing related issues.

Infrastructure

Include information on infrastructure in place to address share technology solutions.

Emerging technology investigations

Are there emerging technology investigations taking place, e.g. Internet and EDI issues.

Applications

Cite application technology solutions, e.g. contact management.

Non-Standard Technology

Point out any "non-standard" technology needs in terms of new or vendor technologies.

First-time use of technology

Cite briefly any first time use of technology affecting the technology landscape.

Vendor solutions

Are there any vendor solutions involved, e.g. third party dependencies?

Potential Key Initiatives

List and describe those major initiatives that did not make the "cut" (could not be funded), e. g., new system, building infrastructure, or significant skills shortfall requiring training. We would expect in the range of two-three initiatives for most groups.

Initiatives	Required Resources		$ Estimated ($000)
	Full Time Employees	Consultants	Total Project
Initiative 1	0	0	0
Initiative 2	0	0	0
Initiative 3	0	0	0
Initiative 4	0	0	0
Initiative 5	0	0	0
Initiative 6	0	0	0
Initiative 7	0	0	0
Initiative 8	0	0	0
Initiative 9	0	0	0
Initiative 10	0	0	0
Initiative 11	0	0	0
Initiative 12	0	0	0
Total	**0**	**0**	**$0**

Insert Key Initiative Name

Description

Provide a brief description of the overall initiative, its overall objectives, and timing.

Business Purpose

Identify the business purpose (e.g., process improvement, product stewardship, call center, financial accounting, etc.).

Initiative Result

Specifically state the system and/or components that will be built.

Impact and Alternatives

Describe impacts if initiatives are not pursued in the coming year, either qualitatively or quantitatively.

Provide alternative plan for launching these efforts given that they may not get attention in the coming year; e.g., feasibility research or vendor assistance.

Appendix A

Glossary

Beta Product or service in period of testing prior to actual production release.

Best Case Schedule Estimates For key initiatives, present the best estimate of when initiative will be completed.

Business Unit's Mission An all encompassing statement on the currency of the organization and a decisive message on where the organization is going. An idea that conjures up in simple form the desires of the people of a particular entity and direction to which they are headed.

Business Unit's Objectives States <u>what</u> is to be achieved and <u>when</u> the results are to be accomplished, but does not state how the results are achieved.

Business Unit's Strategies The <u>pattern</u> or <u>plan</u> that integrates an organization's goals, policies, and action sequences into a cohesive whole.

Business Purpose Purpose for initiative undertaking (process improvement, product stewardship, call center, financial accounting, etc.) Highlight and identify the systems and/or system components that will be built.

Business Sponsor Business Executive accountable and responsible for the planned initiative.

Business Systems Plan Enables the Business Unit to effectively align its system environment and technology strategy with the strategic objectives and initiatives of the business. Method employed by the Chief Information Officer (CIO, to monitor and provide feedback to the Business Unit or Corporate Area relative to their alignment of Business Plans and Systems Objectives.

Call Center Technology Planning, deployment or support systems, facilities and processes designed to receive telephone calls from customer requesting service, information and making a complaint.

Capital Expenditure Includes purchased software, purchased hardware (including PC's and peripherals)
and infrastructure hardware (e.g. wiring). Capital Expense does not include costs of software development for BSP purposes.

Chargeback to Corporate Portion of the information technology budget dedicated to chargeback to Corporate.

Compliance and External Regulatory Initiatives Stategic initiatives that have major compliance and regulatory components.

Computer Telephony Planning, deployment or support of technology which integrates voice communications and computer systems, typically for telemarketing and customer service applications.

Consultants Workers who are not full time employees of the company.

Cost Savings Business justification for an initiative based on cost cutting and savings.

Cross BU initiative Initiative that goes across the landscape of the enterprise. Inititative that might involve technology and business sharing among business units.

Current Year Cost All costs (system, business and operational) associated with the initiative for the current year.

Data Mining Planning or use of techniques (e.g., induction, statistics, neural networks, and data visualization) or tools to extract information from large quantities of data to identify hidden relationships, correlations, or patterns.

Data Warehousing Planning, deployment or support of highly summarized subject-based data stores used for decision support, data mining, or reporting. Data extracted from existing databases and is stored in another location to be used for inquiry and forecasting.

Electronic Commerce Planning, deployment, support, or use of technologies for replacing commercial
  paperflows and staff interactions with standardized electronically implemented processes both within
  and between enterprises.

Emerging Technology *See New Technology.*

Emerging Technology Investigations Technology research that involves analysis, study and examination of emerging technology.

Full Time Employees Employees working in a full time status at over 35 hours per week.

Hurdle Rate Value Business justification for an initiative based on the hurdle rate. Hurdle rate used
  interchangeably with discount rate. This is called the opportunity cost or return forgone by
  investing in one project vs another.   Rate takes into consideration the risk sensitivity of a project.

Image Planning, deployment, support, or use of a set of strategies, technologies, and applications for converting and storing traditional paper-based documents into electronic images for subsequent display, printing or distribution.

Information Advantage - Delivery Strategic themes relationship between initiative
  and ability to creates information advantage based on delivery. State clearly whether the initiative
  creates an advantage for Company X, Inc. through delivery.

Information Advantage - Mining Strategic themes relationship between initiative
  and ability to create information advantage based on mining of information. State clearly whether the
  initiative creates an advantage for Company X, Inc. through mining of information.

Information Advantage - Quality Strategic themes relationship between initiative
  and ability to creates information advantage based on quality of information. State clearly whether the
  initiative create an advantage for Company X, Inc. through information quality.

Information Advantage - Warehousing Strategic themes relationship between initiative
  and ability to create information advantage based on warehousing. State clearly whether the
  initiative creates an advantage for Company X, Inc. through warehousing of information.

Information Technology Budget Information Technology budget that includes monies assigned to all Business Unit's projects including both stategic and business-as-usual initiatives.

Information Technology Initiative Strategic initiative/program driven with information technology as an enabler with a specific purpose to support or enable one or more business objective.

Information Technology Strategy High-level approach, scheme, or tactics developed to support or enable business objectives and strategies.

Infrastructure System back-bone on which all technology efforts are built. (e.g. distributed computing environment, wide and local area network, communication landscape.)

Infrastructure - Desktop Technology Upgrades Strategic themes relationship between initiative and desktop upgrade. State clearly whether the initiative involves desktop technology upgrade.

Infrastructure - Major Increases in Processing Strategic themes relationship between initiative and
  increase in technology processing. State clearly whether the initiative requires a major increase in processing.

Infrastructure - Shift from One Processing Environment Strategic themes relationship between initiative and processing environment. State clearly whether the initiative will result in a shift from one processing environment to another.

Infrastructure Upgrades Change and upgrade to current system backbone on which technology efforts are built. *See Infrastructure.*

Initiative Economics Consists of key financial data for an initiative. Data includes current year cost, revenue contribution, cost savings, total project cost, and capital expenditure, if any.

Internet Technologies Technologies associated with the Internet and the World-Wide Web.

Key Initiatives Key strategic programs and initiatives for the upcoming planning cycle.

Massively Parallel Processing Large Scale Computing Computers constructed from large scale number of separate processors linked by high speed communications. Typically, all processors can communicate with one another and have access to shared I/O devices and or computer memory.

Net Present Value Business justification for an initiative based on the net present value of the project.
Net Present Value defined as accumulated present value of benefit over cost of an initiative.

New technologies New technology which includes current and emerging technology platform (e.g, data mining, internet, fuzzy logic, image/workflow).

New Development Methodologies Processes or technology development that involves the usage of new
development procedure and techniques.

Non-discretionary Funding activities which the Business Unit's has no discretion or choice in making. This normally involves Business-as-Usual and chargeback to Corporate.

Non-Standard Technology Technology that does not fall within the sphere of Technology covered in the Company X, Inc.'s Information Technology Standards.

Operational Goals A picture of where the organization is currently and the progress that is expected to be made during the upcoming year.

Other Development Information Technology development that is not part of strategic initiative development or other discretionary activities creation.

Outsourced Components Components of an outsourcing activity.

Outsourcing Activity that involves the movement of Company X, Inc.'s employees and other resources to an entity outside of Company X, Inc.

Return On Investment Value Business justification for an initiative based on return on investment. Gain over cost on a return basis. Calculated financial return from an investment in a strategic initiatives.

Revenue Enhancement Value Business justification for an initiative based on revenue enhancement.
Launching of initiative will lead to positive increase revenues and cash flow.

Revenue Contribution Highlight, if possible, any revenue that this initiative will generate.

Sales and Marketing - Contact Management Strategic themes relationship between initiative and contact management. State clearly whether the initiative involves contact with the customers.

Sales and Marketing - Information Analytics Strategic themes relationship between initiative and information analytics. State clearly whether the initiative analysis of information that will create
competitive advantage for the Group.

Sales and Marketing - Sales Tracking Strategic themes relationship between initiative and sales tracking. State clearly whether the initiative involves tracking of sales activities.

Sub-projects Projects that are not major initiatives, but are key parts that will lead to the completion of key initiative.

Strategic Development Development of strategic initiatives.

Strategic Necessity Business justification for an initiative based on strategic necessity. Launching of

initiative is due to other than quantitative reasons.

Technology Requirements For the initative, identify the technologies that will be needed.

Total Project Cost All costs (system, business and operational) associated with the initiative over the life of the initiative.

Touching The Customer - Electronic Interaction Tracking Strategic themes relationship between initiative and interaction tracking. State clearly whether the initiative involves electronic interaction
tracking.

Touching The Customer - House-holding Tracking Strategic themes relationship between initiative
and house holding tracking. State clearly whether the initiative involves householding tracking.

Voice Response Units Planning, deployment, or support technologies for voice response applications and
platforms.

Vendor solutions Teechnology that involves interaction with vendors or has any third-party dependencies.

Wireless Communication Planning, deployment, support, or use of system that transfers data via non
-wired systems (e.g. cellular, PDA, PCS, IR, laser, etc.).

Worst Case Schedule Estimates For major initiatives, present the best estimate of when initiative will be completed.

This Page Intentionally Left Blank

About the Author

Rupert Hayles is the Chief Operating Officer of Christ Church, a non-profit organization consisting of over 5,000 members. He provides oversight to the organization's operations and subsidiary corporations consisting of schools, radio and television entity and a community development corporation.

He has dual degrees in Accounting and Management Information Systems and graduate degrees in Finance and Decision Sciences from Pennsylvania 's prestigious Wharton Business School. Mr. Hayles has held several senior level strategic planning positions in the field of Information Technology with Prudential Insurance Company of America, Cytec Industries, Inc., and Merck & Company. A former United States Air Force officer, Rupert is an Adjunct Professor of Strategic Technology Management at Stillman School of Business, Seton Hall University

Mr. Hayles is married to Maryann Hayles and they live in Blairstown, New Jersey along with their two dogs and cat, Giselle, Vladimeir and Zoie.